A PONY FOR SALE

A PONY FOR SALE

DIANA PULLEIN-THOMPSON

Armada

First published in the U.K. in 1951 by
William Collins Sons & Co. Ltd., London and Glasgow.
This edition was first published in 1970 by May Fair Books Ltd.,
14 St. James's Place, London S.W.1.

This impression 1974

© Diana Pullein-Thompson 1951

Printed in Great Britain by
Love & Malcomson Ltd.,
Brighton Road, Redhill, Surrey.

*Facilities for the cover photograph kindly provided by
The Moat House, Benenden, Kent*

CONTENTS

PART I
By Guy Beaumont

PART II
By Pip Cox

PART III
By Lydia Pike

PART IV
By Lettie Lonsdale

PART ONE
By Guy Beaumont

CHAPTER ONE

"TELEGRAM FOR Beaumont! Telegram for Beaumont!" For a moment the voice echoed down the corridors, before growing indistinct in the school quad and finally fading from earshot in the direction of the playing fields. I started. *My* name was Beaumont!

I left the house-room at the double, raced down the Chestnut Walk and found Hatt, a little chap new that term, near the playing fields.

"Oh, here you are! Mr. Storwood told me to give you this. I hope nothing awful has happened," he said.

"Thanks." Mr. Storwood was my housemaster.

I tore open the envelope; the telegram said:

Sherry's filly born to-day—brown with a star. Mummy.

"Okay—good news. My mare's had a foal," I told Hatt.

My mind turned to home; to the red brick manor-house with its musty creepers, the ancient weapons, the antlers and the lone fox's mask hanging in the dark entrance hall and the polo sticks in the corner. To the dusty old stables, the saddle-room and the smell of varnish and leather. To the home fields and the horses in them—Guardsman, Bruno and Sherry.

Brown with a star meant the foal would be like Sherry, who had been one of the best ponies in the county, a brilliant hunter with perfect manners until lamed for life by a nasty fall on a tarmac road. But, having little imagination, I could not picture the foal at Sherry's side, nor galloping in our green meadows, nor lying like a big dog in the lush June grass. I could not picture her at all and, half-term being over, I had to wait till the holidays to see her, which was very hard.

Back in the house-room I told Whipple and Reed, two chaps with homes in the country, about my telegram. Whipple, who had a pony of his own, was interested but Reed only said: "Honestly, Beaumont, your horsiness is getting chronic. Put a gag on it, there's a good fellow, or we'll all turn looney."

I felt like throwing something at him, but instead I said: "You're just wet," and walked out of the room.

Though I curbed mention of my foal in my conversation, I could not prevent myself thinking of her, for I was even keener on horses then than I am now, and I found my mind wandering during games and lessons. On the hot playing fields I thought of point-to-points for it was my ambition to win one. Working in the lab, I planned my foal's education and career.

I renewed my subscription to *Horse and Hound*, which I read greedily, and wrote home for my books on breaking and schooling.

With the help of Whipple, I decided that my foal should be named Martini. Her sire was called Rascal of Rapallo.

At last the term, seeming longer than ever before, dragged to its end, which was celebrated in the usual way with parties, fights and feasts. And on a wet day in late July I was homeward bound in a special train, then dashing across London to Paddington in a taxi and then, as the clerks left their offices and the workmen left their factories and their yards, I reached our nearest town's station. There was Daddy, in breeches, looking every bit the retired army officer, and outside, unchanged but for a few additional chips, was our battered brake. In the front seat sat Random, the old black Labrador that we had had since he was a puppy, who gave me the dignified welcome that befitted his age.

The drive home was like all drives home at the beginning of holidays. I noticed the changes in the countryside, the progress of houses in the process of being built, the growth of young animals that I had seen at half-term.

My father talked of the local horses. Old Shadwell's

10

mare had won at the Three Counties. George Lane's grey had been put in the back line at Dryford. Pam Hill had taken a dramatic plunge into the open water at Little Sanfield. Peter Pope's filly was chasing well and Colonel Nell's Brave Boy was turning out a handful. I listened vaguely. I did not mind much about the successes and failures of these people. In those days I thought mostly of myself, my hopes and ambitions. Besides, I was not very interested in shows; I thought that hunting and point-to-pointing was more in my line.

We turned up the unkempt drive shaded by trees, passed the home paddock where, enclosed by iron railings, Bruno and Guardsman grazed peacefully. Mummy, a tall figure with greying hair, was waiting. She had just returned from a dull and, in her opinion, unnecessary lecture on *leisure* in the village hall. It had been organised by the local branch of the Women's Institute.

"I would have been much better gardening; the rose border is choked with weeds," she said as we hurried round the back of the house to see Sherry and Martini. Mummy has always been crazy on gardening, but she never manages to keep up with the weeds in our garden. Sometimes in the winter she nearly defeats them; the paths and borders are almost clear, but in the spring they return with all the energy of the young and by May they reign triumphant again in half the flower-beds.

The rain had ceased; the land glistened in the pale evening sunlight; across the fields, beyond Frank Smith's copse, the Church's clock chimed six, and I looked down our long meadow and saw at the end of it the brown dot against a green hedgerow, which was Martini.

"How like our horses; if ever you want them they are always as far away as possible," said Mummy.

"They'll come," said Daddy.

I called and Sherry, who was grazing beside Martini, threw up her head. Then I whistled, and Martini got slowly to her feet and the two of them, the mare and the foal, trotted towards us across the meadow. Martini moved

11

well, carrying her head and tail high and showing less knee action than her dam. She had the funny woolly coat that foals are always born with and a tiny well-cut head.

"She's hard to fault, Guy," said Daddy. "Look at her deep girth—plenty of heart room there. She'll stand a long day's hunting all right—got wonderful legs and feet too."

The two of them trotted towards us

"Are you pleased with her, Guy?" asked Mummy.

"She's smashing," I replied, grinning broadly with pride. "A real winner."

Sherry and Martini stopped when they reached us and Sherry searched my pockets for food, while Martini touched my feet and legs with her ridiculously small muzzle.

I had never disliked school, but felt wildly pleased at the prospect of leaving it. But I was very happy now to be back, the long summer holiday stretching before me, with Random and the horses, and later, cub-hunting. Of all my homecomings I remember this one the most clearly. Perhaps it was my happiest.

Daddy had bought a tiny head-collar and put it on Martini.

"Makes her look quite professional, like the foals in the paddocks by Newmarket," said Mummy.

"Now you are here, what about a leading lesson?" suggested Daddy.

"Okay, if you can lead Sherry I'll try to get Martini to follow," I said.

"Well, I suppose I must change and do a bit to the herbaceous border before the sun goes down," said Mummy, wandering away towards the house.

At first Martini would not follow Sherry. She threw up her head, rolled her eyes till the whites showed and planted her four feet firmly on the ground, but when she saw her dam walking away so briskly and confidently she wavered, and a whinny from Sherry settled the matter. Martini plunged forward, dragging me behind her.

After a few minutes we turned the mare and foal loose and paid a visit to Guardsman and Bruno. Guardsman was a black gelding of sixteen hands, two inches, with large kind eyes and a Roman nose. My father was only twelve stone, but Guardsman could have carried fifteen with ease. Bruno was a lightweight bay horse with black points and a thin white blaze; he was fast and a good mover, and had won a few point-to-points in his younger days. They were both well-made with sound legs and feet. Daddy hunted them alternately, except during the Christmas holidays after Sherry's unfortunate fall, when Bruno was put at my disposal. Sherry used to pull out hunting, but Bruno, although willing, was never quite up to the bit. He was very comfortable, though, and if you gave him a very loose rein and used your legs he would be well up to the front, jumping everything in a calm and easy style. He was never so friendly as Sherry, and now he hurried away as soon as he had eaten the carrot which I had given him.

Daddy patted Guardsmen, saying: "This is a good old

fellow, Guy, you know—never saw him take Bradley's brook last season, did you? Pity, he jumped like a six-year-old."

Eventually talking, I suspect, of the horse shows and sales that would take place during the next eight weeks, we hurried indoors for drinks before dinner. I remember that I was allowed a glass of sherry because I was now fourteen, which made the evening seem very special.

"To-morrow we'll get those lazy old horses up and go for a hack, Guy," said Daddy.

"And give Martini another leading lesson," I added.

CHAPTER TWO

THE SUMMER holidays passed rapidly—as all holidays pass if you have much to do—and Martini's hindquarters grew faster than her forehand, so that she looked very peculiar indeed. We taught her to lead well in hand behind Sherry and to allow us to pick up her feet and play with her mane and forelock and bandage her tail. When she was eight weeks old the farrier rasped her hoofs, which were neat and black and hard, for the first time. And shortly afterwards I returned to school and became crazy on Rugger.

In the Christmas holidays Martini was stabled at night and on wet days, but received less attention from me than she had in the summer holidays, because I was busy hunting and helping Dick Warren, our huntsman, exercise hounds. But in the Easter holidays, we decided to enter her in a class for yearlings at a nearby show, so she had frequent leading lessons and was groomed daily. She had left her dam in March and was rather thin at this time, though her coat shone, and each day we gave her a feed of crushed oats which we bought from a friendly farmer.

14

In preparation for the show, I taught her to trot out and to stand properly with her weight equally distributed on all four legs, and to stand still while I ran a hand down her neat tendons.

Then, on a fine clear day in early May I rose at half-past six, when the dew still glistened on the hedges and the birds sang their first gay songs, and groomed Martini. Having slept in a rug and having been groomed regularly for some time, she did not need much brushing. Her dark-brown coat lay flat and shone like polished coffee beans. Her legs were black with no white socks, so I did not have to wash them. I felt light of heart when I left her eventually and returned to the house for a breakfast of porridge, bacon and eggs and toast and marmalade—so essential a breakfast on a show morning.

Martini's class was scheduled to begin at ten o'clock, so it was necessary for us to make an early start. My parents were up and unusually cheerful when I went indoors. They were both coming to the show. They always took a great interest in Martini and were very fond of Sherry, whom Daddy had bought quite cheaply at a sale, for twenty pounds.

At half-past eight the horse-box arrived and surprised Guardsman and Bruno, so that they galloped round the paddock with their tails kinked high up over their backs.

Martini was scared by the box at first, but presently we persuaded her to approach it and then walk, step by step, up the ramp. She looked very tiny and frightened inside and very smart in the brown and red day-rug, which Mummy had made her out of an old rug of Guardsman's, and the small polished leather head collar and white rope.

"I think you've got a winner, Guy," said Daddy, who is always unreasonably optimistic.

"Poor little thing. She looks so pathetic," said Mummy.

Martini travelled well and we arrived at the show at

half-past nine, when the ground was almost bare of spectators and the air was filled with the shrill, hysterical neighs of youngsters parted from their dams or friends. Martini, usually quiet, became hysterical too and kicked the horse-box, and presently, when I led her out, she dragged me around and flung her head about in a wild and frightened manner. Our class was the first. The box-driver came to my rescue and held Martini while I gave her a last brush over and oiled her feet. All my previous confidence had fled and I felt sure that she would behave badly in the ring. I saw some of Daddy's acquaintances and friends, leading or riding superior, highly-bred horses. Martini looked very small and ponyish to me now and, as I led her to the collecting ring, people seemed merely to throw her a glance and then look away again as though saying to themselves: "Ah, she's no good—no need to worry about her."

Daddy had lost some of his optimism too. He would only talk about Colonel Nell's bay filly and Mrs. Dayfield's beautiful chestnut colt.

Mummy hovered by the collecting ring, saying: "Oh, Guy, she looks *sweet*, only so tiny compared with the rest, so slender somehow," at frequent intervals, which, since foals are supposed to have good bone and plenty of substance as well as quality, was not very comforting.

At last we were told to go into the main ring. "Your filly's not bad-looking, you know, but *poor*. Tried any boiled wheat?" asked Colonel Nell, leading the way with his bay.

When people in the world of horses say *poor* they mean thin and inadequately fed and, now that Martini was amongst other ponies and horses of her own age, I realised that her quarters were not round enough and that her neck looked too light. However, she walked gaily with an interested air and she was not by any means the thinnest in the class.

The judges were two farmers who bred horses; one farmer was tall and fat and the other small and wiry. They

16

only seemed to notice Martini when she was looking her worst, which made the last remnant of my previous hopes disappear. She was alternately wild and excited when she dragged at her rope, neighed frantically and swished her tail, and looked sad, tired and depressed, when she dawdled with her head very low as though it was too heavy for her body.

I cannot tell you how many times we walked round that ring, but I remember that an age seemed to have passed when the judges eventually called in the first three horses: Colonel Nell's bay, Mrs. Dayfield's chestnut and a little liver chestnut led by a girl of about thirteen. A long pause followed; the judges seemed unable to make up their minds and the atmosphere grew tense. Martini dawdled and the yearling in front of her bucked. Then the wiry farmer looked at Martini and spoke to his co-judge, who beckoned to a steward who called me into the line.

You can imagine my surprise. When leaving home, I had half-expected Martini to be first or second—so many people had come to the Manor and admired her during the past ten months—but arriving at the show I had lost nearly all hope and had even pictured myself the last and most useless in the back row. Actually, the judges only made a front row, because, I presume, there were only eight entries.

They called in one more competitor as an individual, a brown colt with four white socks, and the remaining three were brought in together.

The judges told Colonel Nell to lead his bay out in hand, and Colonel Nell set us all a very good example by making his filly stand beautifully so that she looked her very best, and walked to the brush fence and trotted her back with the calm and confident air of an expert. Mrs. Dayfield's colt went well also, but the girl's liver chestnut played up and nearly escaped. Presently it was my turn and, attempting to appear confident, I led Martini out of the line and halted her in front of the judges as the others had done. She drooped but, thanks to her earlier lessons, stood with her weight well distributed.

Mummy, in a linen two-piece, and Daddy, sportingly dressed with hacking jacket and buff waistcoat, waved from the ringside. I nodded and turned my gaze back to the judges, who were looking Martini up and down with the intent and critical expression that all judges try to wear.

"Needs a bit more flesh on her," said the thin judge as though Martini were a pig.

"Trot her up," said the other.

She felt gayer when she was trotting and frisked and shook her head.

"Your pony moves quite well," said Mrs. Dayfield in surprised accents when I returned to the line.

We were asked to lead the ponies round once more, in a smaller circle, and then we were called in on the same order as before.

I was presented with a bright green rosette, which said *reserve*, by the little judge. The fat judge said: "Your filly's a bit backward. Pity."

We walked round with our rosettes, accompanied by faint clapping, and were met at the exit by parents, friends, followers or grooms.

"Well done, Guy," said Mummy.

"Put up quite a good show, didn't she?" said Daddy. Random solemnly gave me his paw.

Mr. Cox, a farmer from whom we had once bought a load of straw, approached me. A very small girl with flaxen curled hair hung on his arm. He wore a blue tweed riding coat over grey flannel trousers and had a vague un-farmer-like expression.

"Pretty little thing, Mr. Beaumont," he said, patting Martini and addressing me. "My little girl's quite fallen in love with it, haven't you, Pip?"

The child wriggled self-consciously and whispered: "Yes, Daddy."

"She's shy," said Mummy.

"Speak up—never be a horsewoman if you're afraid of things," said Daddy in bracing accents.

"She's at the awkward age, I expect," continued Mummy sympathetically.

"Well, Guy, I suppose we must be pushing on. Time to go home. No point in staying," said Daddy, who is no conversationalist. We bade Mr. Cox good-bye and I led Martini to the horse-box. It had been a fairly successful day, I thought, although lacking in excitement. Wait till I start point-to-pointing, then all this will seem very tame, I decided.

The horse-box driver pinned the green rosette up in his cab, so that other drivers should see that his charge had been *in the money*, as he put it, and then he helped me to persuade Martini up the ramp again.

As we left the show ground I saw Mr. Cox's daughter gazing after the horse-box, a tiny figure with flaxen curls and a pale face.

"Well, you didn't do so badly, Martini," I said.

CHAPTER THREE

THERE IS nothing of importance or interest to record of Martini's life between the age of one and four years. I am afraid that my enthusiasm for riding and horses died down during this time, so that she did not have as much attention as she deserved and needed. But, when I left school at seventeen, I had seven months' holiday before going to Sandhurst and, having spent my foreign currency allowance at Easter, in Brittany, I decided to stay at home and break and school Martini.

I had little experience in training young horses then and, having no faith in my father's advice, which was obviously out of date, I asked Maurice Treadwell, who was going up to Sandhurst with me and was also taking a long holiday, to stay at the Manor and help me with Martini. I have always respected his opinion where riding and horses are concerned, because he had made a study of them. At the age of seventeen he was an impressive horseman; he had attended dressage and show-jumping courses under a Continental instructor, and had won second in a strong novice dressage class, with a six-year-old that he had broken and schooled himself. As a child he had jumped successfully in some of the stiffest competitions in the country: and he could be justly described as a "hard man to hounds"!

He arrived on a wet day in May with enough trunks for a whole family's clothes. Apparently he had brought four pairs of boots, complete with trees, so that he would be ready for any emergency.

"Five months is a long time to stay with anyone. After all, you never know; I might be asked to show a hack, when I should need my *Peal* pair, or be offered a mount for cubbing, when I should need my best brown pair; or one of your friends might be in the soup and want to borrow some boots—then I could help them out. It's no use leaving clothes at home when you go away to stay or you're bound to want them," said Maurice.

He liked Martini; he was a lightweight and always admired ponies with quality. She was in the stable, fat and sleek now and very graceful-looking.

"What do we do first? Long reining?" I asked. "I haven't any long reins, by the way."

"I don't think that's necessary, you know. The things you teach a pony on the long reins can be taught as well, if not better, from the saddle, and why walk if you can ride?" said Maurice.

"All right. How do we start? Lungeing?"

"I think that's best," answered Maurice. "At least, we get her used to wearing a saddle and bridle at the same time and then, in about a week, we back her. That is if you agree. I don't want to run your show."

"No, but I don't know much about breaking, as I told

you. I can stay on fairly well. I mean I can keep up with hounds and jump most things that come to me. But I don't know anything about this schooling and dressage you are always talking about, and if Martini is going to be sold to a nice child, as I hope she will be, she must be fairly well schooled, mustn't she?"

"I should say so," said Maurice. "Dressage is only training, you know. Every horse of reasonable conformation should be able to do elementary dressage. It's just a matter of suppling them, teaching them obedience and developing their muscles."

"I doubt that old Guardsman and Bruno could do it," I said. "But come in to tea. We can start on Martini afterwards."

We returned to the house and ate a country tea of bread and butter, and Mummy's home-made crab apple jelly and fruit cake, and then hurried back to the stable to start Martini's education. Maurice held her in a head-collar, while I saddled her very quietly, being careful to put the saddle well forward before sliding it into place, thus ensuring that the hairs underneath were lying flat. She stood quietly without showing signs of fear, and presently we led her round the loose-box a few times and then Maurice suggested that we should bridle her, so I fetched a rubber snaffle, and she made no fuss at all about being bridled.

"So far, so good," said Maurice.

"We mustn't speak too soon," I warned him.

"I think she's going to be all right, you know. Aren't you, Martini?" said Maurice.

Presently we took off the tack and buckled the lunge-rein, that I had bought specially for Martini, on to the head-collar. Then I collected an old driving-whip, which was to substitute a lungeing-whip, and we proceeded to the paddock, from which Guardsman and Bruno had been removed.

It was one of those lovely warm, fragrant May evenings. The apple trees in our garden were bursting into bloom; the air was fresh and sweet after recent rain; the green

21

turf in the well-grazed paddock was soft and springy underfoot; from nearby meadows came the scent of hay and meadowsweet.

Following my instructions, Maurice took the rein first and I led Martini round him three times, stopping her when he said "Whoa" and leading her forward when he said "Walk on." She took no notice of him at all, and soon I stepped back and left her to her own devices. She tried to follow me, was pulled up short by the rein, and then turned in and walked boldly up to Maurice.

"No luck," he said. "No rewards yet. Out you go. Walk on." He pushed her away from him and made a triangle, with Martini, the whip and the rein as the three sides and himself as the apex. Martini stopped and he tapped her with the whip and clicked his tongue, again saying "Walk on." She hesitated, looked at him and then obeyed. A moment later she stopped but a stroke from the whip sent her round again. Soon she had walked round several times without any hesitation, and Maurice said "Whoa" and "Come here," and tempted her to walk in to him, rewarding her with a handful of oats.

"Your turn now, isn't it, Guy?" asked Maurice.

"Yes, I'll have a shot," I said, taking Martini from him.

Maurice had lunged her to the left, so I decided to lunge her to the right. I was not at first successful, because she disliked the change of direction and wanted to turn back the other way, but eventually, with Maurice's help, I managed to make her do as I wished by walking a smaller circle myself, so that the whip was always just behind her.

After five minutes I called her in and rewarded her, as Maurice had done, with a pat and a handful of oats. Then we turned her loose with Sherry, who was very old and doddering these days, and returned as dusk fell to the house, to talk of hunting and point-to-pointing and dressage.

Next day we repeated the lesson, and the day after we lunged her in a saddle and bridle at the walk and trot, and led her along the grass verge by the road to look at the traffic. Daddy was rather sceptical about our breaking-in methods. In his younger days he had made use of the army rough-riders and he thought we were very slow, but Maurice put forward some very sound arguments. So, without any real opposition we put off the backing for several days, till Martini was dead quiet to be saddled and bridled and would stand still while we put weight in the stirrups and pressure on the saddle.

Then, one May morning of alternate showers and sunshine, we backed Martini in her loose-box. Maurice held her head while I slowly mounted, lowering myself very gently into the saddle. She twitched back an ear and I spoke and patted her. Presently Maurice led her round the box a few times, then I gave her a handful of oats from the saddle. She nibbled my boot, and I dismounted her from the other side, and rode her round the other way.

Daddy's head appeared over the stable door.

"Oh, so you've backed her at last," he said. "She looks quiet enough."

"Yes, everything's going to plan," replied Maurice.

"No need for army rough-riders yet," I added. "Let's lunge her now. Are you going to watch, Daddy?"

Just because Daddy was watching, Martini gave a fine display of bucking on the lunge-rein and nearly pulled me over. Maurice said I should find it easier to hold her if I put my hand against my hip. Daddy said I must be sure she respected me, and Mummy, who was watching while she gardened, said I must be careful—it would be terrible if my front teeth were kicked out.

During the next two days we took it in turns to lead each other round the paddock on Martini and agreed that she felt very hesitant and unbalanced. But Maurice said that all youngsters felt uncertain, unfit and unbalanced the first times they were ridden.

On the third day I rode Martini while Maurice lunged her, and I learned what an important part lungeing plays

23

in the breaking of horses. As Maurice pointed out, it not only supples, balances and makes them fit, but it teaches the words of command, which are a tremendous help when you are first using the aids. Now, riding Martini on the lunge-rein for the first time, if, squeezing with my calves, I found she did not walk on, I had only to say "Walk on" loudly and clearly for her to obey me at once. Stopping was the same; if closing my legs, shutting my fingers and slowing up my body so that it no longer moved with my mount did not stop her, I had only to say "Whoa" to be brought to a standstill immediately.

A week after Martini was backed, Maurice and I had started to ride her round the paddock at the walk and trot on our own, and she had almost learned to to turn on the forehand. Then we had her shod, which took the best part of two hours, because she played up in the beginning, and we took her out on the roads with Guardsman. Then I started to meet Daddy's local friends and they all gave me advice. One told me to ride Martini in a twisted snaffle; another told me to give her plenty of jogging on the hard roads—"give her plenty of work, if you don't want any trouble." A third said I must not give her more than forty minutes' riding a day or she would develop splints. I believe that I might have wavered and taken somebody's advice, though none of them had any right to give it, had Maurice not been there. Maurice would listen to them in silence, almost a respectful silence. Afterward, when we had ridden away from them, he would pull their theories, if you could call their suggestions theories, to pieces with scorn. Not that Maurice was conceited about his riding; he wasn't. He knew his own shortcomings all too well; he had had them pointed out to him by some of the finest horsemen in the land. But he could not bear to hear people holding forth on some subject about which they knew next to nothing.

These rides along the country roads, down shady lanes through green June woods, by the side of hayfields, with Guardsman and Martini were very pleasant. Maurice and

I would generally change mounts half-way and, at this time, it would be a pleasure to change from Martini, who dawdled, shied and tripped, to Guardsman with his long stride and purposeful walk. But gradually, as June changed to July, Martini became a better ride. She grew more attentive to the aids. She carried her head higher and she saw fewer bogies in the hedges. And as she improved and became fit, we started to school her in the paddock. We hacked and schooled on alternate days and lunged her twice a week. We had given her her first canter up a hill during one of her early rides, but we still postponed cantering her in the paddock.

"We must get her tempo at the trot right first," said Maurice.

I could never quite understand his theories on tempo then, and they used to drive Daddy mad.

"Tempo! Lot of nonsense! What that mare needs is livening up—a few gallops. She's idle, bone idle, Guy. Can't see that all this trotting round and round the paddock will do her much good," he would tell us.

Maurice would remain quite calm and obstinate.

"Well, we will see," he would reply.

Sometimes Maurice's calmness and patience would exasperate me, but I can see now that it was those qualities which made him so good with difficult or nervous horses; patience, calmness and imagination.

Martini seemed lazy in the paddock at first, but this was mostly due to unfitness and the fact that her muscles were undeveloped. We gave her balancing exercises, such as the diagonal change of hand, the counter change of hand, and halting, backing and turning on the forehand. We made her trot as slowly as she could down the short sides of the paddock and then increased her speed till she was trotting as fast as she could without losing balance on the long sides. We rode her in circles. We taught her to open gates, and we started to teach her to canter and jump on the lunge-rein.

Maurice was determined that we should not hurry her.

"If we ask too much of her, work her too hard, we shall only make her develop splints or spavins or curbs. She'll grow sour too, and probably her back will become rigid into the bargain," he said.

I shall never forget those mornings spent in the paddock. We were terribly enthusiastic, but sometimes we quarrelled. Maurice often criticised me when I was riding and I was supposed to criticise him, but I found little to correct in his riding and he constantly accused me of not watching him properly. Now and again I became irritated by his flow of instruction and started a row, but Maurice never seemed to lose his temper, so that I always got the worst of any argument.

Daddy and Mummy say Maurice was a prig in those days, but if he was I never noticed it. I only knew that he was marvellous with horses and so, although I might be annoyed by his corrections at the time, I actually paid great attention to them and he did much to alter my seat and leg position for the better and to interest me in the finer points of horsemanship.

By the end of August we had started to canter Martini in the paddock. She was very unbalanced and leaned heavily on the bit, but each week she showed improvement and she rarely led off with the wrong leg. Gradually we increased the length of her lessons in the paddock till, at the end of September, they lasted an hour and twenty minutes, which included half an hour's cantering.

I never realised how happy those hours in the paddock were until Martini was sold and I no longer had a pony to school, nor a friend at home to criticise me. There is something marvellous about training horses. Maurice says there is a quotation from somewhere which says *it is better to travel hopefully than to arrive*, which perhaps explains the great pleasure that dressage experts derive from that unending training which they give to their mounts, that striving for a perfection that is never attained. I am far from being an expert, but since I first knew Maurice I have always tried to improve my mounts, and I think that is where the fascination of riding lies with me now.

Daddy is different. He likes riding because it is good for his liver, because he feels healthy and fit after a brisk hack in the country. He likes hunting for the same reason and because he enjoys the social side of it and because he has the competitive spirit and considers his presence in the first flight to be a triumph.

In September he urged us to cub-hunt Martini, but we started to teach her to jump and waited till October, when she would pop over a fence of two feet quietly and neatly. She learned, also to behave well when other horses galloped by her.

Maurice and I agreed that cub-hunting is meant for the training of young hounds, not horses, so we were determined that Martini should be reasonably sensible.

"It would be terrible if you kicked or trampled on a hound. The Master would never forgive you and, as co-trainer, I should feel a terrible sense of responsibility," said Maurice.

But as the leaves scattered in their thousands, turning the roadsides brown, red and gold, our hopes grew and we rang up the Master, chose a meet and asked his permission to bring Martini.

CHAPTER FOUR

THERE ARE some days that are engraved on one's memory for ever. There may be no reason why this should be so. They may have been quite unimportant days, full of trivial happenings, and yet one cannot forget them. The Friday on which we went cub-hunting was like this.

We rose early on one of the greyest and warmest autumn mornings and stole downstairs, along the garden path to the stables. The air was close and clammy, the skies low and heavy, and cobwebs hung on the damp hedges. The horses and Martini were surprised to see us at this unusual hour. We were taking the three of them, for we were all hunting—Daddy, Maurice and I.

We fed, mucked out and groomed in silence except for an occasional word to a horse, because Maurice never speaks much before ten o'clock. He and Daddy used to be awful at breakfast; they would each disappear behind a paper and only grunt when I spoke to them. Mummy is always late in the morning, so I had to resort to the papers too.

On this Friday, though, they managed to talk a little as we ate a large meal of porridge, haddock, toast and butter and marmalade. At least, Maurice only ate the third course; an inability to eat a decent breakfast being another of his early-morning faults. I remember the conversation perfectly.

"Cubbing, Guy," said Daddy, "is the finest thing in the world. Jolts the liver, clears the brain and livens the appetite."

"Hmm," said Maurice from behind a sporting paper. "I see Dick Warren won the Open Hunter Trial at Oakfield. Quite a good show, you know."

"Do you think scent will be good?" I asked.

"Scent? When Where?" asked Maurice.

"To-day, of course."

"Oh, bound to be. Just the morning for a good day's cubbing, there's no doubt about that," said Daddy. "How's Guardsman, by the way? Ready for the fray?"

"His usual solemn self," I replied.

"Good old horse that, Maurice, bold, wise and as hard as nails. He wouldn't be easy to replace," said Daddy.

"No, he's a useful sort and well mannered too," said Maurice. "I see Song of Dawn won last week."

They both disappeared behind papers again.

"It's nearly time to go," I said, giving Random my toast crusts. Daddy heard the dog's teeth scrunching.

"I wish you wouldn't feed him at table, Guy. You know I don't like it. He'll be getting fat and start begging at meal-times. I can't stand dogs doing that. It's making fools of them, too," he said.

"Sorry," I said. "Let's go."

Half an hour later we were on the road, with a four-mile hack to Valley End in front of us. Daddy was riding Guardsman, Maurice Bruno and myself Martini. The horses walked well and I had difficulty in keeping up with them. I remember that I was afraid Martini would be tired before we arrived at the meet. It was so muggy that one could not feel energetic, and after a while I let her go at the pace she liked. Daddy said she was idle and needed the stick. Maurice said she was unfit and could not help herself.

Nobody likes being left behind, and I felt annoyed with both of them. I dawdled along in silence and tried to think of other things. Presently we rode through an old and picturesque hamlet; the sort of hamlet that is loved by tourists, particularly Americans. Ducks ran in front of us across the narrow road; a dog in a cottage garden choked and barked at the end of a chain; a shire horse plodded by with nodding head, a sleepy labourer sitting sideways on his back. And then, ahead, we saw the hounds, a melée of black and tan, lemon and white; a flash of scarlet on a grey horse. I felt that thrill, that catch at the heart which I suppose I shall always feel to the end of my days when I see a pack of hounds. My feeling of annoyance vanished; my energy revived. I was filled with pleasant anticipation and a feeling of happiness.

Martini wakened as though from a dream. She pricked her little brown ears, raised her head, kinked her tail. And then she snorted like a wild horse on the prairies.

Guardsman and Bruno gave each other a knowing look; they were too old and wise to make a fuss.

We trotted, and at last Martini was a real pleasure to

ride, and I realised how much she had learned during those hours in the paddock. She was excited; she wanted to catch up with hounds, but she did not pull. She collected, dropping her quarters, using her hocks, flexing at the poll and relaxing her lower jaw. She was lively and keen, but as light as a feather. Between my hands and legs I held a vast reservoir of energy. It was a new and wonderful feeling. For the first time I understood some of Maurice's theories.

"It would be worth showing that filly next year, she's going like a show pony, Guy. Shouldn't be surprised if she was in the money more than once. Carries herself well," said Daddy.

"Pity she's not a hand taller, or she would make a dressage horse, you know," said Maurice. "Her tempo is all right now. She moves well and her conformation is good."

When we reached Valley End, a small straggling village with hills rising steeply on either side, we found quite a large gathering outside the Three Bells, a long, low, white inn with green windows and a beautifully kept garden. Amongst this gathering were several of Daddy's friends and acquaintances, and they hastened to comment on Martini's appearance and manners. She was still excited, refusing to stand still, and presently she broke into a sweat.

"I'm glad to see you've got a bit more meat on that youngster of yours. Looks better, doesn't she? Might make something nice in time," said Colonel Nell.

"What's that you are riding to-day, Guy?" asked George Lane. "Not a bad sort of pony. How do you like my new brown? He won at Studwell last week. Old Jim Watson said he had given him a wonderful ride."

"Oh, Guy, what a dear little thing! How old is she? I think she's *sweet*," cried Pam Hill.

"Yes, she's going fairly well now. It's a pity she isn't taller or she'd make a dressage horse," I said.

"Dressage! You keep off dressage, Guy," said Colonel Nell. "Steer clear of it as you would the plague."

"Why? It's only training. I want Martini to have good

30

manners, so I'm teaching her elementary dressage. I think it's a first-class idea," I said.

"The way to teach a horse manners is to give him a hard season's hunting. There's nothing like it. Do ten times more good than all the circus tricks, people call dressage, in the world," retorted Colonel Nell.

I looked round for Maurice. I wanted his support, but he was busy talking to a farmer on a stout little cob. I felt lost, unequal to taking a creditable part in the argument. I paused.

"Well, take my advice, Guy, and don't mess that pony about with a lot of dressage," said Colonel Nell, and he swung his horse round and rode away.

"What's that, Guy?" said Daddy approaching. "Getting some useful hints from the Colonel? You take notice of him. He knows a thing or two."

A moment later hounds moved off and Maurice joined Daddy and me.

"Martini is behaving well, isn't she? You know, that schooling in the paddock has improved her head carriage tremendously, hasn't it?" he said.

There was a large field, considering that we were only cub-hunting, and we made a fine clatter on the road to the first covert. Faint sunshine broke the greyness in the eastern sky, but moisture still clung to the grass, the trees and the hedgerows, and the air was damp and close.

"A good scenting morning," said Mrs. Dayfield, trotting past me on a light bay thoroughbred which Maurice said would make a dressage horse.

We turned off the road into a stubble field; the first whipper-in galloped ahead to the left of a covert of firs; the second whipper-in had ridden on earlier to the far side. The Master decided to make the field spread themselves out on the right side, which was the longest. We were told to tap our saddles and turn back any cubs that appeared.

With a cheery voice the huntsman threw his hounds into covert. Martini grew very excited; she backed and pawed the ground and, when a hound spoke and the huntsman doubled the horn, she bounded forward, nearly unseating me. I was between Daddy and Maurice, but they were both far too busy tapping their saddles and watching for cubs to notice my difficulties. A moment later Martini neighed and I was glad that we were not hunting properly, when you must be so very quiet at covertside. Then Daddy yelled: "Hike back, Charlie," in a most professional voice, and I saw a cub dash back into covert.

The Master, who was at the end of our line, at the corner where he could see the downward side of the covert, turned the same cub back a few moments later. His action was followed by a crash of hound music which made Martini plunge and buck, and stirred me to the heart's core. I am not very interested in houndwork. The main pleasure I derived from hunting in those days was the fun of galloping and jumping over farmers' land and fences.

A point-to-point would have pleased me as much, except for the absence of the music of hound and horn, and now I longed for a fox to leave covert and run out into the open fields. My longing was answered very soon. Hounds lost the cub and found the line of an old fox, which dodged the first whipper-in who was the wrong side of a fearsome barbed-wire fence, ran across a newly-ploughed field, through a spinney and down a steep hill into the valley.

Hounds followed in full cry; the horn rang through the woods and cheered them on. Deadly still, the Master waited till they were out in the ploughed field, then he led the way through the covert at a hand gallop. It was nearly the beginning of the hunting season and he had decided that we should forget the cubs and have a good run, and as we pelted down the treacherous hill into the valley I felt glad of his decision. Hounds had swung left at the bottom, and we could see them crossing a stubble field. They were running well together. A sheet could have covered them, to use a hunting expression. And they gave us a fine burst of hound music. The first whipper-in was on the ground, opening a large wired gate for the huntsman, who was blowing the gone-away. We clattered across a lane and then the Master, who was at the head of the cavalcade, jumped some post and rails of about four feet into a meadow adjoining the stubble field. Daddy and Maurice followed, but it was too high for Martini. I knew that I must not overface her. If Maurice had not been present I might have had a shot, but with him looking on I dared not try. To him, overfacing young horses was a crime at least equal to petty thieving. Sick at heart, I turned away.

"Bad luck," called Maurice.

". . . Might find a gap farther along," shouted Daddy.

"Why not have a shot?" cried Pam Hill, riding her roan mare with great determination at the post and rails. Her mare refused and I hurried away down the lane. It was bad enough to lose hounds, but worse to lose them in the company of Pam Hill, whose ceaseless chatter and bumptious manner are unbearable in any cicumstances.

I turned my attention back to the stubble field. The huntsman and whipper-in were through the gate and in pursuit of hounds, who were entering a copse at the end of a long green meadow crossed by a narrow stream. I trotted up the lane. Martini was reluctant to leave the other horses and neighed forlornly. Feeling unreasonably annoyed with her, I used my whip. In spite of my years and the fact that I had another month's hunting in front of me, I felt sick with disappointment. I heard the other riders, who had been stopped by the post and rails, turn their horses and ride away in the opposite direction from that which I was taking. The horn grew faint, and gradually faded from earshot, and, with sinking spirits, I looked in vain for a gap in the stubble. I thought of my father and Maurice enjoying the run, jumping enormous fences on Guardsman and Bruno. And then I

33

B

We galloped with the wind

heard hounds again. They were turning back. Each moment their cry grew louder and each moment my hopes rose higher.

I stopped Martini and looked forward up the lane, and presently a large dog fox crossed over and entered a spinney of firs. Hounds were very close now, right on his line. A view holloa was unnecessary and would have disturbed them, so I rode Martini on to the bank, took off my bowler and pointed it in the direction of the spinney to indicate to the huntsman, who was a couple of fields away, where the fox had gone.

Hounds checked for a moment in the firs and then picked up the line again and, in full chorus, pushed the fox out into the open. Martini leaped off the bank and stood trembling like a leaf, in the lane. A field away, the huntsman blew his horn and cheered hounds forward. The followers were straggled out behind, the Master in the lead. I felt a peculiar kind of thrill as I rode Martini through the open gateway and past the spinney in the wake of hounds. I felt it was my duty to keep in touch with them. When the huntsman caught up I would drop behind again. We galloped with the wind; the only horse and rider on the right side of the lane. The turf flew up behind us; a few curious crows circled above us; a herd of cows looked on with bovine interest. I said aloud—goodness knows why, for I'm not fond of poetry—"I am the master of my fate: I am the captain of my soul," and put Martini at a thorn hedge of about three feet. I believe she was as excited as I was. I remember she never hesitated, but just lengthened her stride and jumped like an old hand at the game. We landed in time to see hounds bowl over their fox. Regent and Fancy were in the lead, with Echo and Harmony close on their heels. A farm labourer, who had been ploughing with a pair of horses, reached them before I did and cut off the mask, brush and two pads. The huntsman arrived looking very hot, with a scratch across his face, a few minutes later. I dismounted and loosened Martini's girths.

35

"Regent and Fancy bowled him over," I said. The huntsman said that they were a good couple of hounds and not many packs in England could go like this one, a statement which I did not consider to be strictly true. The farm labourer said his employer would be glad to hear that we had killed the blighter, who had raided his chicken house a week ago. While the huntsman encouraged the young hounds to take an interest in the remains of the fox, I led Martini back towards the spinney, because horses hate the smell of blood.

Presently the field came over the hedge and thundered across the plough.

"Well, Guy, you seem to have had the best of it, after all," said Daddy.

"Martini was going well, wasn't she? I saw you in the distance sailing the hedge," said Maurice.

"Quite a useful sort of filly that," remarked Colonel Nell.

"Are you thinking of selling her?" asked George Lane.

"Not yet," I said.

Dismounted, we ate our sandwiches. Steam rose from our hot horses; plough clung to our wet hunting boots; hounds started to roll and then to wander off. At last the sun broke right through the clouds and lit the damp brown countryside.

"I'm going to find Martini a really good home," I said, and I meant what I said.

CHAPTER FIVE

MAURICE LEFT a few days after the meet at Valley End. I hunted Martini twice during November and, on both occasions, she went extremely well. Then, because my long holiday was nearing its end, I advertised her for sale.

Martini, dark brown mare. Four yrs. 14.2. By T.B.,
Rascal of Rapallo, out of New Forest mare. Broken and
schooled by owner. Hunted and goes well. £100..

My address was at the bottom. I was not satisfied with
the advertisement, but I could think of nothing better. I
wished that Maurice was still staying at the Manor,
because he would have helped.

Colonel Nell told me that it was the wrong time of year
to try to sell ponies. The market was down. I should have
waited till March. Mrs. Dayfield said I was asking too
much for Martini, and George Lane said I was asking
fifty pounds too little.

But on Saturday evening three prospective buyers rang
me up. First of all, a Mr. Smith-Jenkins, who wanted a
hardy pony for his little girl of nine who stuttered. She
was a complete beginner and he hoped riding might help
to cure her stutter. I told him that Martini was unsuitable
for beginners and too young to know how to cure
stutterers.

Then a well-known dealer, quite a giant in the world
of horses, rang up and asked whether Martini would win
pony showing classes. He was looking out for a mount
for a famous child rider—he mentioned her name—but
it must be absolutely first-class, up to White City and
Richmond standards. And I had to admit that, as far as
showing was concerned, Martini was only second-rate.
He was disappointed, said that one hundred pounds was
a lot of money to ask for a second-rate four-year-old, and
rang off.

For a moment I felt depressed and then the telephone
bell rang again. This time it was Mr. Cox, who reminded
me that I had talked to him three years ago when showing
Martini.

I racked my brain for one frantic moment and then
remembered him and said: "Oh, yes, how do you do?"

He told me that his daughter, Pip, had never forgotten
Martini and had been very excited when she found the

pony advertised. Pip had really grown out of her old Dartmoor and needed a second pony. Would mine do? Was it quiet? asked Mr. Cox.

I hesitated and recalled a tiny figure with flaxen curls watching a horse-box leave a show ground. She would be fond of Martini, I thought.

"Depends on how well your daughter can ride," I said.

"Yes, of course," said Mr. Cox. "Pip's quite a good little horsewoman. She's ridden since she was six. She's had Rex, our old Dartmoor pony, you see. She's a game kid, though she looks so slight, and her heart's with ponies."

I thought of a small red heart lying in a wet field with a decrepit Dartmoor pony.

"Well, would you like to come and see and try Martini?" I asked.

We fixed that the Cox family should come on Sunday afternoon and then we rang off.

Mummy said she remembered Pip as rather a sweet little girl, and Daddy said Mr. Cox was quite a sound sort of chap, though he didn't know much about farming.

Next morning dawned crisp and clear. A far-away sun looked down from blue skies to a white and frozen world. Guardsman and Bruno were filled with energy, and banged their doors and called for their breakfasts in a manner that ill-befitted their years. Random frolicked in the drive like a puppy, and I groomed Martini vigorously for close on an hour. She was not clipped, but she had worn a rug since early autumn and her coat was soft and shiny. I was looking forward to my army career, but I was very sorry to lose such a good pupil and friend as Martini, and my thoughts were not happy ones.

By lunch-time the ground had thawed. The sun was still shining and it was one of those bright, invigorating days with a sharp nip which sets the blood tingling. The sort of day that Mummy and Maurice hate and Daddy and I love.

At two o'clock sharp the Coxes arrived. Mr. Cox was

tall and vague with pale-blue eyes, and Mrs. Cox was fair-skinned, soft-featured and plump. Pip had grown of course, but she was still pale and fragile-looking, and flaxen curls framed her rather characterless face. She was attractive though, and had pleasant blue eyes. I could not imagine her losing her temper with an animal.

Martini was very friendly and nuzzled the Coxes' pockets. I felt quite proud of her as I took off the rug and revealed her shining coat, long sloping shoulder and round quarters.

"Hasn't she got a pretty head? So intelligent," said Pip, in a small voice.

"And lovely slender legs," added Mrs. Cox, who obviously knew very little about ponies.

"Up to plenty of weight," remarked Mr. Cox in a knowing voice.

"Now, remember, Pip, if we buy Martini for you, we won't get you another present when Christmas comes," said Mrs. Cox.

"I wouldn't want anything else, Mummy. When I've got Martini I shall be satisfied for ever and ever," said Pip, burying her head in Martini's mane.

"Never known a kid set its heart on anything like Pip has on your pony," said Mr. Cox with a laugh.

"Won't old Rex be pleased to see her? He's been so lonely all these years," said Pip.

"What a large step up it will be, won't it? Martini's nearly a horse. You will be able to see over all the fences and hedges," Mrs. Cox told Pip with a faintly patronising smile, which I guessed she generally wore when talking to children.

The Coxes seemed to have decided to buy Martini whatever happened. I thought otherwise. I wanted Martini to have a good home and I wanted to be sure that Pip could ride her.

"I'll fetch Martini's tack, if you will excuse me a moment. I think you had better try her in the paddock," I said.

I put on her saddle and double bridle.

"Does she pull?" asked Pip in a whisper.

If she had been a boy I should have told her to speak up, because her tiny voice and habit of whispering were getting on my nerves. But I told myself to be tolerant, because she was a girl and, after all, horses like quiet people.

"No, Martini goes quite nicely," I said. "She's very light really and a straight mover."

"She's got a good, kind eye. I like to see that in a pony. Means you can trust them," said Mr. Cox.

"Though Rex has a wicked little rolling eye and behaves beautifully all the same. I don't think anyone could make him be naughty. Dear old Rex!" said Mrs. Cox, turning to me.

"Oh, really?" I said, leading the way to the paddock.

Martini went very well. Pip had very well-cut riding clothes and the two of them made a pleasing pair. I could imagine them winning equitation classes and I could imagine their photograph in the paper. They both looked so neat, so well turned out—although I should not boast about Martini's appearance, having groomed her myself.

I felt very sorry to lose such a good-looking pony, but I felt glad that she was being sold to Pip, who would obviously appreciate her, and would keep her for years and years. For Pip, I decided, would never grow too heavy or too big for Martini.

"She's certainly a pretty pony, isn't she?" said Mr. Cox.

"And doesn't she suit Pip?" asked Mrs. Cox, as Pip cantered Martini in a circle.

Then Daddy appeared on the scene and shook Mr. and Mrs. Cox firmly by the hand.

"That's a rattling good pony, as kind and sensible as a pony can be. Never turns a hair out hunting and goes all day without tiring. If I had a grandchild I should buy Martini for it without a moment's hesitation," he said.

While Daddy and the Coxes talked, I watched Pip riding. She was rather too passive for my liking, though she sat beautifully and Martini seemed happy. I wished Maurice was here to advise me. He would have known what was wrong with Pip at once.

I asked her if she found Martini a good ride and she gasped: "Oh, she's lovely! So easy to stop and start and not nearly so bumpy as Rex."

I suggested a low jump, and Pip agreed and rode Martini rather timidly at the low rails in the paddock. Martini approached cautiously—I think she was trying to be careful of her new and very light rider—lengthened her stride a few yards away and popped over the rails very neatly. Pip lost a stirrup.

"Well done!" called Daddy.

"Oh, dear, she's so different from Rex, who cat-jumps. But she's lovely and I shall soon get used to her," said Pip, retrieving her stirrup.

"I think you've ridden for long enough now, haven't you, darling? We can't take up all Mr. Beaumont's time," said Mrs. Cox.

"Don't worry about me. I've got plenty of time to spare," said Daddy and I almost at the same moment.

"Would you like to try Martini on the road, by the way?" I asked.

"Your father says she's as quiet as a lamb in traffic and I'm sure we can take his word for it, thank you very much," said Mr. Cox.

We walked back to the stable-yard in silence. I felt depressed about losing Martini so soon, although I knew that I should soon be absorbed in other interests.

Pip unsaddled Martini and put on the rug, because Mrs. Cox wanted to be sure that she could manage her in the stable.

"Of course, there will be the men on the farm to help her, but I would so much rather she did it all herself," said Mrs. Cox.

"Quite right," said Daddy."

"I love Martini's star," said Pip.

41

"When can we have her?" asked Mr. Cox.

"As soon as you like. Isn't that right, Guy?" said Daddy.

"Perfectly," I answered, thinking that this deal was over too quickly. I had expected that Mr. Cox would have asked me to take less. Surely there was always a little beating down attempted when horses changed hands?

"Oh, to-morrow, please, Daddy," pleaded Pip.

"Now don't be impatient. You must see when Daddy can arrange it," said Mrs. Cox.

"I'll have a word with Ted Wallis to-morrow. I expect he'll manage Tuesday, would that be convenient for you?"

Ted Wallis owned a cattle-truck.

"Yes, quite," I told Mr. Cox.

They left at last, after giving me a cheque for one hundred pounds; a pink piece of paper which looked a poor exchange for Martini.

"Now, keep that money. Hang on to it and spend it later on a horse, when you are commissioned," advised Daddy. I settled the horses and went indoors.

Much to my surprise I slept all night without waking or dreaming. Next morning I took Martini for a last ride.

She went beautifully. Never before had she seemed so light in hand. Never before had she gone so well between my hands and legs. Never before had I appreciated her so much. Now she was a far better ride than Guardsman or Bruno. She was fit and gay and obedient. She was supple and brisk and well balanced. I felt that I had given away a jewel, a friend and a companion. But then I believe that one never appreciates anything to the full until one is about to lose it.

I rode for two hours through silent, muffled woods, across open meadows, where the east wind blew in my face and brought tears to my eyes, down quiet country roads, along little twisty lanes and, at last, home in the sunlight across a glorious stretch of common. And, all the time, my heart said . . . this is the last ride, the last

42

ride. . . . This is the last ride. . . . And then Martini's hoofs beat the same words; the wind whistled them across the open fields; the telephone wires hummed them; and the village bus groaned them as it climbed Bramble Hill. I felt sadder than I had felt before in my life. But I consoled myself with the thought that I would soon recover from my sadness and that Martini would be very happy with Pip, who deserved a good pony.

PART TWO
By Pip Cox

CHAPTER SIX

I COULD hardly wait for Tuesday, when Martini, my Christmas present, would arrive. I longed to see her at Bannisters Farm, which lies snug and small and neat, like a toy farm, in a valley approached by a rough and rutted lane. I longed to see her installed in the large airy loose-box which stands by our small modern farmhouse. I could imagine her pretty head, with the sweet white star, looking out over the cream-coloured door. I could imagine my friends admiring her. . . . No one, I decided, could help liking Martini. She was so well bred, so graceful and elegant, and so nice-tempered. Tessa, my special friend at that moment, would love her at once. Miss Stallwood, the owner of our local riding school, would surely think her well made, and my father's farmhands would think her smart.

Of course I would always love Rex; he was so fat and round and funny, with wicked rolling eyes, which belied his good nature. I hoped that he would like Martini and not be jealous. He must understand that I was growing too big for him, although last summer we had won a few rosettes in riding and showing classes. He was supposed to be twenty years old, but he looked less.

At last Monday was over and I went to bed, and then it was Tuesday and Mummy said that I could stay at home instead of going to school, so that I should be able to greet Martini.

I hung about the farmyard all morning, but Martini did not arrive until after lunch, when I had decided to sit indoors and read a book.

She had sweated a little in the cattle-truck, but she looked lovely as she pranced down the ramp like a startled thoroughbred in a picture. Daddy took her from Ted Wallis and put her in the loose-box. She looked over the door and neighed, and became so excited that we had to shut the top door in case she might try to jump out.

I had meant to ride her, but Daddy said she seemed too upset. I had better try her tomorrow. I wailed that I would be at school then and hoped that Mummy would say that I could stay at home again. But she didn't; she said I must wait till Thursday, which is only a half-day.

Poor Martini was very lonely on Wednesday, according to George, who looks after the cows, and she banged her door and walked round and round her box like a caged wild animal. I could barely attend to my lessons at school, I was so busy imagining my ride next day.

And when it came it was a lovely ride, which fulfilled my expectations, my wildest hopes. The air was sharp and cold, following a morning of wind and rain. Pools of water were in the fields and the gardens and at the roadsides, and they reflected like mirrors the blue sky and high-flying clouds. An eastern breeze shook the rain from the branches of the bare December trees, and there was a freshness about the day and a cold clarity about the sky that was very pleasant.

There was quite a gathering of people to see me set off on this first, and therefore exciting, ride. I will admit that I was not a little nervous, not exactly of Martini but of circumstances, of all the things that might occur to spoil the day.

George had helped me with the saddling and bridling and insisted on holding Martini now while I mounted, although, thanks to Guy Beaumont's competent breaking-in, she would stand still when told.

My parents, my Aunt Mary and my friend Tessa watched.

"Smashing little mare this," said George.

"You look very nice. Doesn't she, Daddy? Don't you think so, Mary?" said Mummy.

"Quite the little horsewoman," replied Aunt Mary.

According to Tessa, I squirmed. I did not like my aunt's condescending tone of voice.

"Just trot her round the meadow a few times, dear, before you take her out on the road," said Mummy.

Tessa had brought over her grey pony, Squib, and she decided to ride Squib with me now.

We trotted and cantered in the meadow and Martini felt wonderful, although she was certainly fresh and wanted to gallop.

"You *are* lucky," said Tessa. "Be a sport and let me have a ride on her."

I hesitated. Not because I thought Tessa was incapable of managing Martini; but because Mummy says her hands are heavy and I did not want to annoy my parents. Tessa, however, dismounted without waiting for an answer.

"You can have Squib," she said.

We changed mounts and I was able to see how well Martini moved. Tessa was more reckless than I had been and galloped round several times.

"She's simply wonderful, isn't she?" I said, when Tessa came to a halt.

"Abso-bally-lutely."

My parents came from the gate.

"Don't you think you had better go now? Or you won't be back before dark," said Mummy, and I knew that she had not been pleased to see Tessa riding Martini.

Presently we were on the road. Daddy's last words were still ringing in my ears . . . "Now be careful, Pip. Remember it's your first ride. See that she doesn't do anything reckless, Tessa."

As though I *ever* did anything reckless! I thought. Usually he says I haven't any drive. At shows I'm always feeble in events that need recklessness. Oh, why do I feel a tiny bit nervous now? Why can't I be determined and brave like Tessa?

We had planned to take Martini to Elm Tree Riding School to see Miss Stallwood, which meant nearly an hour's ride. I wanted to go quietly, but Tessa was cold and wanted to hurry. I expect she was right really. It *was* best to hurry, but I felt cautious.

Martini felt strange after Rex. Not only was I farther from the ground, but between my hands and legs I seemed to hold a mass of potential power. I only had to relax, while trotting, for a moment and the power would be released and we would be galloping, galloping probably faster than I had ever galloped before. I could stop along on Rex and think of other things, but I had to concentrate on my riding on Martini. I had to be awake and alive and yet very quiet and still. I felt that I had never ridden so well before, but it was an effort at the trot and canter, and I wished that Tessa would walk.

Soon I felt I could bear it no longer, and I plucked up courage and told her that she wasn't being fair on Martini, who wanted time to take in her new surroundings.

My excuse worked, to my surprise, and we walked.

"By the way, what was Guy Beaumont like? I've heard he's rather stuck up," said Tessa.

"No, not at all. I thought he was jolly nice and he knows an awful lot about horses," I replied, recalling a tall dark boy with a quiet voice and nice brown eyes. "He's got rather a nice house and stables and two ever such nice hunters," I added.

"You don't say!" said Tessa.

I couldn't think why she had a down on Guy Beaumont, but later I learned that he had told her off in the hunting field for pressing hounds, and Tessa doesn't like being corrected or ordered about. She has drive and determination. That's why my parents think she is a good friend for me.

We reached the Elm Tree Riding School as the Brakely church clock struck three. It was a dismal place; dank, damp and dreary, with too many trees hiding the tell-tale sunshine that would have shown the dinginess of the windows more clearly. Everyone worked very hard at the

Elm Tree Riding School. The horses were let out to hire at all hours of the day to anybody who liked to pay for them, whether they were tired or not, and the horses and Miss Stallwood taught scores of children to ride. And yet, in spite of their work, the place looked poverty-stricken. The yard needed re-gravelling; the doors and windows needed repainting; the track was old and cracked. The horses lived in pre-war portable loose-boxes with inefficient chalk floors and warped walls. They were all very kind, quiet and gentle, except for Tom Tit, a snappy chestnut gelding, who kicked and bit. I learned to ride at the Elm Tree Riding School, and I like Miss Stallwood, who was always patient and hard-working.

She came out of the saddle-room, where she had been cleaning tack, at the sound of our hoof-beats.

"Oh, hallo, Tessa. Hallo, Pip! I thought you were Mr. Mildway, the young man who's taken out my Duchess this afternoon. He's due back now."

"I thought you would like to see my new pony," I told her.

"Oh, she's rather a dear, Pip. And nicely put together too." Miss Stallwood stood back and looked Martini over with a critical eye as she spoke.

"Daddy thinks she will win showing classes next summer. I'm awfully excited, though I don't expect I will ride her as well as Guy Beaumont did. She's sweet, though, isn't she?" I said.

"She's certainly fit and she's got a bit of blood about her. The only thing is—are you sure you can manage her? She's obviously highly-strung," said Miss Stallwood.

"That's what *I'm* wondering. You are a bit nervous sometimes, aren't you?" said Tessa.

"Only a *tiny* bit very occasionally. Mummy says I will grow out of it," I told them.

"That pony needs a good rider. She's very different from your old Rex," said Miss Stallwood.

"Abso-bally-lutely!" said Tessa.

"Would you like a ride on her?" I asked Miss

Stallwood. Miss Stallwood is a good instructress, but nervous. She looked a little apprehensively at Martini and then refused my offer.

"I would like to see *you* ride her in the paddock," she said.

"All right," I agreed with trepidation, because their remarks had suddenly made me lose confidence.

I turned Martini round and then, to my great relief, there was a clatter of hoofs and Duchess came trotting wearily up the drive ridden by a young man with a loudly checked coat and riding boots with spurs.

Miss Stallwood said: "Oh dear, I must see to my client now. We had better leave the ride in the paddock for another day."

The young man dismounted and handed his reins to Miss Stallwood.

"The old mare seems very slow today," he said, looking at Duchess's heaving black flanks.

"You had better try Tom Tit next time. He's got more life in him. Poor old Duchess feels her years, I'm afraid," said Miss Stallwood.

The young man had turned his eyes on Martini. "I say, that's a nice little mare. A blood 'un, isn't she?" he asked.

"No, she's a half-bred," said Miss Stallwood.

"She's spirited, I should say. Can I have her next time? Tom Tit's rather on the narrow side for me and I really like something with a bit of life."

I felt sorry for Miss Stallwood. It was bitter for her that the only animal he admired belonged to someone else.

"No, I'm afraid not. The pony belongs to one of my pupils, you see," she said. "The girl who's riding it."

"It's getting dark. I think it's jolly well time we left," said Tessa suddenly.

Miss Stallwood, a bent, weary figure in a dust-coat, led Duchess into a loose-box.

"Goodbye, children. Come again. Take care of that pony, Pip, she's worth it," she said wistfully.

Tessa shot off down the drive on Squib, and Martini followed at a jog-trot. The young man's eyes were on Martini and I felt proud of my new pony.

"Steady, please," I called to Tessa, as she trotted on ahead down the road.

"What's the matter? We've got to hurry if we are going to be home before dark," she retorted with hardly a backward glance.

Martini must have grown cold standing in Miss Stallwood's yard. She was certainly glad to be homeward bound now. She wouldn't walk; she cantered sideways and turned her quarters out into the traffic until I just *had* to let her catch up and trot beside Squib.

"I don't see the point of dawdling home. It's getting so beastly dark, too. What's up with you? You are not frightened of Martini, are you?" asked Tessa.

"No, of course I'm not."

"I was only just wondering. 'Cos if you are, I'll ride her for you if you like, and you can have Squib."

"Don't be silly," I said.

The rest of the ride back was lovely. Tessa had been right. It was best to trot most of the way. The ponies seemed happy and we kept warm. Martini was fresh but controllable. Her long easy strides seemed to eat up the miles, and her high head carriage and light mouth were a constant source of joy to me.

The evening grew dark and eerie. Strange shadows lurked amongst the trees. Strange noises broke the stillness, but on Martini I felt safe. The night held no fears for me.

For the first time in my life I felt that I could ride as well as Tessa. When I reached home I was very happy. I told my parents that Martini was the most adorable pony in the world. And lying in bed that night, I planned a rosy future for my pony and myself.

CHAPTER SEVEN

WITH ME at school, it was difficult to keep Martini exercised, but she was not clipped, so in the end we decided to turn her out in the daytime to exercise herself, and I rode her at the weekends and on my half-day. She was generally very fresh, and once nearly ran away with me when Tessa galloped on ahead with Squib. After that incident I hacked alone, when she was much quieter.

Then came the Christmas holidays. The weather was perfect for riding; fine, clear and unbelievably warm. I rode every morning and started to practise jumping Martini in the meadow. Daddy put up a low bar and a pair of hurdles and I managed very well with these, till Tessa came over to lunch two days before Christmas.

"I like your jumps," she said, gobbling bacon and eggs. "May I try Squib over them?"

"If you like, certainly," I replied.

"Show Tessa how Martini jumps," said Mummy.

"She's been out this morning. She may be tired," I said doubtfully.

"Oh, go on, Pip. She's not tired. *Do* show Tessa," said Mummy.

"The pony's going well now. Best buy I've ever made," said Daddy.

The jumping was not successful. I had known in my bones that it wouldn't be. Martini was over-excited. She saw Squib refusing the hurdles and began to twirl round and round. Tessa is a determined but wild rider. She shouted at Squib and used her legs vigorously and waved her elbows, but Squib dodged by each time.

"It's no good," she admitted at last. "*You* have a try. I'm longing to see Martini jump.

"She's all het-up. I don't know that I will," I said.

"Oh, you *must!* You've got to! I've come over especially to see you."

"All right then."

Martini was walking backwards. I loosed my hold on the reins and sent her forward, pointing her at the hurdles. From the first we were not in harmony with each other. I felt insecure. I gripped the mane to give myself confidence. Martini swerved one way and then the other and then galloped past the hurdles, turned left and stopped in front of Squib with a jerk.

"Hard luck! I should have another shot," said Tessa.

"I don't know. She's over-excited. I think I'll leave it till tomorrow."

"Oh, but you can't *possibly* do that. It will be *frightfully* bad for her."

I wanted to say that I knew best what was good for my own pony, but I had not the courage. I looked down at Martini's mane in a frenzy of indecision.

"I believe you are nervous. Shall I have a shot on her?" offered Tessa.

"No, thanks."

Hot and angry, I turned again towards the hurdles. This time I'm going over, I thought, but, after a few strides, Martini hesitated and my heart failed me. I grabbed the mane, gripped the saddle hard with my knees and hoped for the best. For a moment the hurdles loomed before me, then Martini dodged, galloped past them and took me back to Squib.

"*Do* let me have a shot, *please*," pleaded Tessa, dismounting.

I looked towards the meadow gate. My parents weren't there. "All right, but please be careful of her mouth," I said.

In the first attempt Tessa was as unsuccessful as I had been. In the second she jumped the hurdles. I was not surprised, because I knew in my heart that she was a better rider than myself.

"There! Good girl! Good Martini," cried Tessa, breathlessly dismounting.

I wished I had the courage and confidence to mount Squib and put her over the hurdles. Then I would have been quits with my friend. But I hadn't, so that was that. I smiled politely about Tessa's triumph.

"I think you need to kick more, that's all," she said.

"Yes, I expect so," I agreed.

Presently Tessa left and I settled Martini for the night. It was the first time that she had played me up and I felt sad. I expect I'm feeble, I thought, walking in to tea.

My parents asked if I had had a nice ride in the meadow and I had to confess about my incompetence.

"You must put more vigour into your riding, Pip," said Daddy.

"Never mind, better luck next time," said Mummy consolingly.

"By the way," said Daddy, "a card came from the Hunt by afternoon post. The meet on Boxing Day is at Longhatch, so you can go."

"Oh, goody!" I said, picturing myself on Martini galloping with ease across open fields in the wake of hounds.

"What a good thing I got your breeches back from the cleaners yesterday," remarked Mummy.

Christmas passed like a flash, to use Tessa's words. And then it was Boxing Day. I wakened early, full of happy anticipation, and with the kind help of George prepared Martini for hunting. She was a sweet pony to groom; gentle, friendly and obliging. You could not be afraid of her in the stable. George did the difficult jobs like picking out her feet and plaiting her mane. He had once worked in stables so he knew all about it. By nine o'clock she was looking lovely. Her dark-brown coat shone like polished oak and her eyes were bright and gay. I gave her a final stroke with the rubber and went indoors to change my clothes.

Longhatch was only two and a half miles from home,

and Tessa and I started at a quarter past ten, our hopes high and our pockets full of sandwiches.

It was a wild morning, windy and wet. The ponies bowed their heads before the rain. Cars swished by, splashing us as they passed. The air smelt of warm, wet earth and woods and hedgerows.

I had exercised Martini on Christmas Day in the hope that she might be quiet hunting, but this morning she seemed fresher than usual. Somehow she had sensed that something exciting was going to happen. Tessa said she looked lovely, like a pony in a picture.

We found a large gathering of horses and riders at the crossroads where the meet was being held. In spite of the weather most of them seemed cheerful. They were joking about Christmas celebrations.

"Well, John, and what time did you crawl upstairs last night, I mean this morning?" called out a young man on a chestnut.

"You don't say you *managed* to get home in the end," said one middle-aged woman to another.

"Poor old Skylark, I wonder he can carry you. All that turkey and plum pudding must add on nearly a stone, you know. You'll break his old back before you've finished."

"Well, Celia, how are you? A bit 'morning after the night beforish,' I suppose. My dear! My head! I thought the room would never stop going round when I stepped out of bed this morning."

Tessa and I stood together by the signpost. It was ten to eleven and hounds had not arrived yet. Martini had become calm quite suddenly; she stood now with drooping head, resting a leg. Presently Mummy and Daddy arrived and then, a moment later, round the bend came the hounds. The loveliest sight in the world. Scarlet coats and white ties, prancing horses, with jingling bits. Smiling hounds, with waving sterns and, behind, the winding road curving upwards to the woods, warm and

57

brown against the cold, grey sky. It had stopped raining and the wind had dropped.

When the pack and hunt staff had joined the gathering at the crossroads, I called to Trooper, Rex's and my favourite hound. He is lemon and white, the palest in the pack, and he has large and flopping ears and doleful eyes. He put his paw on my stirrup and I talked to him, till Mummy reminded me that I had not yet said good-morning to the huntsman.

At half-past eleven we moved off to draw the first covert. Tessa insisted that she and I should be well to the front, so, although we were only children, we rode directly behind the Master.

Martini was excited. I could feel her quivering, but she didn't pull and I felt quite safe and secure. Several followers told me that she was a nice-looking pony and I found it pleasant not to have to look up to everyone. Rex is very small and nearly all my life I had hunted on the smallest pony in the hunt.

Hounds found immediately they were thrown into covert, and very soon we were all galloping across some open country. I had no choice but to be in the front, because Martini took charge and kept just behind the Master. I lost Tessa and Squib and I lost all sense of direction. The air was cold in my face and brought tears to my eyes; mud from the Master's horse spattered my clothes. I had never ridden so fast before and, to tell the truth, I was a little scared. I wondered what would happen when hounds checked. Would I be able to stop Martini? Or would I ride over Regent or Rapture or Serpent or Truthful? And then we came to a hedge and I grabbed Martini's mane and held my breath. The Master's bay took the hedge like an old hand and Martini followed. I landed just behind him.

"Keep off my tail," he shouted, looking back. I let go of the mane and managed to turn Martini a little to the right, so that we were now galloping to the side of the Master. Hounds were a field ahead, running silently. The huntsman and a whipper-in had to stop for a gate. They left it open and the followers pelted through, the Master shouting: "Last through shut the gate, please."

We crossed a ploughed field and then, ahead, there loomed a row of post and rails, about three feet six in height. They were more formidable than anything that I had ever jumped before. I knew I couldn't stop Martini, so I grabbed the mane again and hoped for the best. She lengthened her stride, took off and cleared the rails with ease. I heard a horse fall behind me.

We were climbing uphill now. At the top hounds checked for a moment and then swung right-handed into a fir copse. The Master steadied his horse and I pulled on my reins, and to my surprise Martini responded at once and we slipped back behind the bay again.

The huntsman was in the covert encouraging his hounds. "Bet the blighter's gone to ground," said the Master to no one in particular.

He stopped his horse and Martini stopped beside him. I felt very conscious of the fact that I was only a child and should, therefore, be at the back. But I was glad that Martini was standing so quietly and I was afraid that if I moved her she would become upset and would misbehave, so I stayed very still where I was listening to the other riders coming up the hill.

Presently a hound gave tongue, then another, and another, and a moment later they had left the copse in full cry. The Master sent his bay into a gallop and Martini followed without hesitation.

We tore down a steep and rather frightening hill, jumped a stile into a wood at the bottom and galloped down a leafy track, at the end of which we found the huntsman refusing a stake and bound hedge.

"Here, Tom, out of the way. I'll give you a lead," shouted the Master. He put his bay over the hedge and the huntsman's black cob followed. Martini snatched the reins from my hands and took me over too. I lost a stirrup and bruised my nose on Martini's neck. If I had been on

Martini snatched the reins from my hands and took me over

Rex I should have stopped to recover, but on my new pony I could not. She galloped on with the other two horses and I was powerless to stop her. We crossed a strip of parkland studded with rabbit holes. Each moment I was afraid that Martini would put a foot in one of them and turn a somersault, but we reached the other end without mishap. We went through a gate which the huntsman opened; crossed a road and entered a wood, where we stopped to listen, for we could no longer hear hounds.

"They are in here somewhere," said the huntsman.

"Did I hear a noise? Ssh a moment," said the Master.

"That's them all right, sir," said the huntsman, sending his cob into a gallop again. We pelted up the wood, through the undergrowth amongst the trees—I expected to bang my knee against a trunk at any minute—and found hounds casting themselves in a ploughed field at the far end.

"Hold hard!" shouted the Master, for behind us we could hear the thundering hoofs of the other horsemen.

I stopped Martini and watched the huntsman take hounds to the hedgerow on the far side of the field and cast them. They picked up the line at once and we were off again. Over the plough, through a gate, down a lane for a few yards and then over a small hedge into a meadow and away into the open country again. There was no checking Martini; she was beside the Master's bay again and her long easy strides seemed to eat up the miles. She was lathered with sweat, covered in mud, but still game. The wind was behind me now bringing with in the sound of following hoofs. I felt a wonderful but rather frightening sensation of speed. I was growing tired. I was afraid that I should fall off if we turned a corner sharply, and I held a lock of Martini's mane to give me confidence. I couldn't see a fox, only the huntsman and hounds, but I wondered if they would kill. I thought I would like to be first on the scene. My parents would be so pleased and they would never be able to say that I was feeble or nervous again. But I wished that the hunt would end quickly. It was awful feeling that I couldn't stop Martini. If I met a barbed-wire fence I might gallop into it, or supposing I slipped a little round a corner and half-fell off, leaving a foot in the stirrup, she wouldn't stop and I might be dragged. There might be a fatal accident. I almost wished that I was struggling along in the wake of the field on Rex again; dear, safe, obliging Rex.

Four meadows with convenient gaps and gates brought us to a narrow spinney, where hounds had checked.

The huntsman hitched his cob to a bush and entered the spinney on foot. Presently we heard him blowing long and dolefully on his horn.

"Gone to ground," said the Master, dismounting.

"Oh dear," I said, because I couldn't think of anything else to say, dismounting also and loosening Martini's girths. At that moment about twenty members of the field arrived. Several of them praised Martini.

"That pony's worth her weight in gold," said a fat elderly woman, in ratcatcher.

"She's very sweet," I replied.

"Jumped like a stag," said a farmer.

"I think I shall go home now. Can you tell me the way back to Bannisters Farm?" I asked.

The farmer knew the way and I left at once. It was only two o'clock and hounds were going back to draw two fields of kale, but I was tired and I wanted to be well on the road for home before Tessa arrived. Tessa always liked to stay out to the bitter end, and she would be sure to try and make me stay out with her.

Martini was terribly excited and wouldn't walk a step of the eight miles to Bannisters Farm. She snorted and sidled and jogged and, every now and then, she neighed for all the horses that we had left behind outside the spinney. I wished for Rex again, and I wished I didn't feel so stiff and sore, and I wished that I was at home eating tea after a glorious hot bath.

CHAPTER EIGHT

TESSA WAS surprised and, I am sorry to say, a little hurt by the way I had deserted her out hunting.

My parents, who, before leaving for home, had seen hounds find and force their fox into the open country, were pleased to learn that Martini had kept me in the first flight. Daddy said he was glad that I showed some signs of possessing *guts*, and Mummy said: "You'll soon be quite notorious, dear; the fastest woman to hounds in the county."

I told no one that I could not control Martini, that I had been afraid.

Two days after that memorable hunt, Tessa rang me and suggested that I should ride over to Miss Stallwood's with her.

"I want to go, because I think I need a lesson," she said.

I knew this was not entirely the reason. The day was Wednesday and on Wednesdays Miss Stallwood's noisiest pupils ride. Tessa wanted to see them again. She likes a rowdy time and misses school in the holidays.

"I expect you'll be pleased to have some useful advice about Martini," she added.

"Okay, I'll come," I said.

The hack over to Elm Tree Riding School was heavenly. Martini was fresh, but very sweet and obliging. Tessa talked all the time, asking questions without waiting for answers, so I was able to give all my attention to my riding.

When we eventually arrived in the damp and shabby stable-yard, we found Miss Stallwood still grooming muddy ponies—she is always behind time—and a small crowd of pupils, including Tim and Peter, Tessa's special friends, watching her.

"Hallo, Tessa and Pip. The new mount looks well. I hear she went like the dickens on Monday," said Miss Stallwood.

"Abso-bally-lutely, left poor little Squib and me miles behind; jolly mingy," said Tessa.

"Oh, poor little Tess, how very sad," said Tim mockingly.

"Can I help at all?" I asked Miss Stallwood, who was looking even more weary and wispy than usual.

"It's very nice of you, dear, but I think I can manage," she said.

"Are you going to ride with us, Tess? Oh, how awful, I think I shall be sick," cried Peter.

"Oh, you're just barmy," retorted Tessa.

"The barmiest boy at the Elm Tree Riding School. Isn't that right, Miss Stallwood?" shouted Tim.

"What did you say, dear?" asked Miss Stallwood, emerging from the saddle-room with a bridle.

"Oh, nothing, only that Peter is barmy," said Tim.

"When on earth are we going to start riding? It's twenty past ten now," said Peter.

"Shall I put on Duchess's bridle?" offered a fair girl with plaits, called Mary.

At half-past ten the class started. We filed out into the paddock. Tessa, Tim and Peter at a fast trot, the rest of us at a walk.

Martini was very excited. She snorted and kinked her tail, and picked up her feet very high.

Miss Stallwood stood in the middle of the paddock and told us to walk round her.

"Oh, silly old schooling! I wish we were going out for a ride," said Tim to Peter.

"I'm tired of dawdling around. I'm going to trot. Come on, Flash, you slow old thing," said Peter.

He was in the lead so we all trotted, and occasionally

Miss Stallwood corrected one of us in rather a tired voice.

"Toes up, Mary. . . . Elbows in, Tim. . . . Kick Duchess, dear. . . . Toes up, Tessa, and you too, Pip."

No one except Mary and myself paid much attention to her remarks. Tim and Peter continued their shouted conversation, and Betty and Megan, who were sisters of twelve and fourteen years, obstinately rode with their toes pointing to the ground.

Presently Tim suggested a canter and we cantered round. Martini livened up and I found her hard to hold. Soon I had passed everyone and was in the lead, and then I caught up with Megan, the last of the line, and rode just behind Tom Tit's Tail. I was afraid that he would kick Martini or myself.

"Take your hands off your pony's neck, Pip dear," instructed Miss Stallwood, and in vain I tried to obey her, but each time I lifted a hand I felt insecure so I had to put it back to keep my balance and give myself confidence.

"Pull her up," said Tessa, who was in front of Megan.

"I can't," I told her. Eventually, to my relief, Miss Stallwood told the class to walk and then to stop, and Martini stopped when Tom Tit stopped.

"Are we going to have competitions now?" asked Tessa.

"Can we have a relay race?" shouted Peter.

"Oh, no! A touch corner race, *please*, Miss Stillwood," pleaded Tom.

"I want to bend," said Megan.

"That's only 'cos Tom Tit's the best bender in the stable," said Tim.

"Not bending. Flash is so awful at it, so slow," said Peter.

"I think we will begin with a ride and lead race," said Miss Stallwood.

"Oh no! Jane is so huge. It takes me ages to mount her. It isn't fair," declared Tim, who was riding a thin old hunter of sixteen hands.

C

"Well, let's start with a relay, then," suggested Miss Stallwood.

"Ow, how unfair. Peter always gets his own way!" said Tim.

"Please be quiet. We will have a touch corner race as well," compromised Miss Stallwood.

"And bending?" asked Megan.

"We'll see."

The relay race was not a success. There were two teams of three . . . Peter, Tim and Tessa, and Betty, Megan and myself. None of the horses except Martini wanted to leave their friends and go across the paddock by themselves. Flash put up a stubborn fight, taking Peter back to Jane and Squib three times, before giving in and trotting across to the far end. Duchess would only walk and Tom Tit kicked Squib. Martini was the last to go in my team. All I was supposed to do was to gallop to the hedge, touch it with a stick, gallop back and pass the stick to the leader, Megan.

Unfortunately Martini became over-excited and wouldn't stop to allow me to pass the stick, but galloped round and round the paddock.

"Oh, come on," shrieked Megan. Our team was in the lead at that moment.

"Pull. Stop her," yelled Betty.

"Lift your hands off the neck," shouted Miss Stallwood.

"We're winning! We're winning!" shouted Tim.

"Lift your hands off the neck, Pip dear," said Miss Stallwood again.

"Oh, come on, Pip!" shrieked Megan.

"Do stop. Don't be feeble," called Betty in despairing accents.

"We've won! Finished! Finished, Miss Stallwood," yelled Tim.

"All right. I've heard. Do try, Pip. Lift your hands off the neck," she said.

I tried, but was too insecure. I felt I *must* lean on my hands. It was all very well for the others to say I was feeble, they didn't know how unseating Martini could be when she galloped. She was so fast and bouncy, quite different from Rex and Duchess and Flash, who hardly dragged their legs off the ground. I wished I had Rex now. He was so good at relay races, so sensible and obliging.

Martini seemed to be increasing speed each moment. At every corner I thought I would fall off. And then suddenly she turned towards the other ponies. We reached them in a matter of seconds, and the next thing I knew was that I was on the ground and Miss Stallwood was saying: "Are you all right, Pip?"

For a moment the paddock went round and round.

"Yes, thank you. Only a little dizzy."

"Well, come and sit down and rest a little, dear."

"Thank you."

Tessa had caught Martini. "Hard luck," she said.

"Surely you could have pulled harder?" said Tim.

I walked away and sat on the fence and held Martini, who seemed rather subdued. I watched the touch corner race and wished that I was a more determined character. I'm just weak-minded, I thought, although, of course, I have no desire to look like Megan and Tessa or to possess their loud, commanding voices. They will grow into awful women, I decided, so organising. No one will want to marry them.

I was glad when the church clock struck twelve and Miss Stallwood said: "I'm afraid it's time to stop now. Come along."

Back in the stable-yard, Tim asked: "Still feeling dizzy?"

"Not really, thanks, but I'm going home. Coming, Tessa?"

"Not yet. What's the hurry?"

"I'm tired," I told her, and then I thanked Miss Stallwood, who said was I sure that I was quite all right, and mounted Martini and left.

For a while I was happy to be alone with my thoughts and Martini, and then I began to feel lonely and friendless. I was disappointed with myself and my pony, and I was a little afraid. Supposing Martini ran away again? On the roads or in the hunting field? Or even now in the woods? What should I do? I would be powerless . . . I would hurt myself against a tree. . . .

I shortened my reins and pushed my feet home in the stirrups, just as a precaution. Best to be prepared, I thought.

My action seemed to upset Martini. She jogged and I shortened the reins again and gripped the saddle hard with my knees.

"Walk, please. There's a good pony," I said in what I hoped were soothing accents.

Martini tossed her head and tried to canter. We were nearly home now and would soon be on the road again. I must quieten her, I thought, I don't want to get tangled up with the traffic.

"Steady, steady," I whispered, but without the desired effect for Martini broke into a slow canter. And then a terrible thing happened; a dog ran out of some bushes and crossed the path behind us, sending Martini into a frenzy of fear. She plunged forward, snatching wildly at the reins and throwing me on to her neck. I grabbed the mane as she broke into a gallop. This is the end, I thought. If it's not the trees, it's the road, the buses and the lorries. . . . Shall I throw myself off? . . . No, I can't; she's going too fast. . . . Oh dear, why didn't I stick to Rex?

I gripped with my knees and hung on to the mane like grim death. We reached the road. If I fall off now I shall really hurt myself, I thought. . . . This is terrible. . . . She's really bolting! Oh, why did I let Tessa persuade me to go to Miss Stallwood's? I knew in my bones that something awful would happen.

On the road, Martini turned for home. Her hoofs made a resounding clatter, bringing people to their windows and doors.

"*Please* stop. Please, Martini. Whoa, whoa, steady," I pleaded.

And then I saw the fields of home, the rooftops of Bannisters Farm, the garden fence. A car passed us slowly; a motor bike whizzed by. Then Martini swung up the drive and galloped me to her stable door and stopped.

It was lunch-time and nobody was about. My parents had not heard the tell-tale hoof-beats. All was quiet; even the pigs seemed to be sleeping. I dismounted and put Martini in her loose-box, which George had prepared for her return. Having unsaddled and bridled her, I went indoors. My parents were eating lunch. I told them of my fall at the Elm Tree Riding School, but omitted to mention my terrifying gallop home. I was too disturbed and upset to be hungry, and I ate even less than usual.

CHAPTER NINE

I WAS horrified when, at tea, Daddy said: "Well, it seems as though you can get one more hunt on Martini before term begins."

"The Meet next Saturday is at Littleworth-on-the-Green," explained Daddy.

I was silent; the memory of my last hunt was strong in my mind. I could not have stopped then if I had wanted. It was only luck which had prevented me from coming to grief; luck and Martini's liking for the Master's horse. Supposing next time I was not so lucky? I might gallop into a wire fence or a rabbit warren and come an awful cropper. I might not be able to get my foot out of the stirrup. I might be dragged. These dreadful possibilities occupied my mind while I ate iced cake and drank tea. I did not want to take Martini to Littleworth-on-the-Green, but I dared not tell my parents.

"You don't sound very thrilled, Pip dear," said Mummy.

"Are you going to show the field the way again?" asked Daddy.

"Yes, yes. But I feel dizzy. It's after my fall this morning. May I leave the table and go upstairs, please, Mummy?" I said, and as I spoke I began to feel tired and a little faint.

"Oh, dear, why didn't you say? Did you hurt yourself this morning? My poor Pip, you must lie down and rest. I'll come up with you and fetch the aspirins." Mummy, all sympathy, left the table and together we went upstairs.

But I did not sleep well that night, nor the next, nor any night before the dreaded Saturday. And yet I was too cowardly to tell my parents of my fears. Each morning I hacked Martini by myself, at a walk, on the roads, for I did not want to risk her bolting with me again. Tessa did not ask me to accompany her on any rides—much to my relief as you can well imagine. My parents had not the slightest suspicion of the true state of my mind. They alluded to me as the "fastest woman over timber in Barsetshire" and as their "dashing daughter," and spoke of Martini with the greatest pride.

And then, all too soon, Saturday arrived; a crisp bright day with the glitter in the skies and a sharp wind whistling on the hill-tops. I knew in my bones that something awful would happen. I wakened with a feeling of catastrophe, and contemplated feigning a tummy-ache; but that, I decided, would only put off the climax. I would always be frightened of Martini, I would never learn to control her, and the sooner my parents learned that dismal fact the better.

Littleworth-on-the-Green was three miles from home, so I set forth at twenty minutes past ten.

Martini was, as I feared, very fresh. She was filled with the joy of living and her own good health, and ready to break into a gallop at the slightest excuse. I kept my reins short and gripped hard with my knees, ignoring her

70

tossing head, and we arrived at the Meet without mishap.

Miss Stallwood was out with Peter, Tim and Megan, and I learned from them that Tessa was in bed with a cold.

Hounds were already on the green, gathered round their huntsman and watched by the two whippers-in. The wintry scene reminded me of a Christmas card and set Martini quivering with excitement. I realised with dread that she anticipated another thrilling gallop. When hounds moved off to the first covert, she took me to the forefront of the field and refused to walk.

"That's a hot pony," said the Master.

"Game as they make 'em," said a fat man in a cap.

"She's young," I gasped, taking another pull at Martini's mouth.

But worse was to come. This time hounds did not find at once. It was a large covert and the huntsman used his voice and horn more than usual. And each time the horn rang through the wood Martini began to paw the ground and tremble with excitement. Then she began to back, and she backed into a smart lady on a large dapple-grey horse, who was very angry. I had to kick Martini to stop her backing and then she plunged forward.

"Can't you control your pony, miss? Keeps on getting in the way," said a farmer.

"Sorry. She's so excited," I gasped, and I felt near to tears.

"I should dismount, dear," advised Miss Stallwood.

"What a barmy animal!" said Tim.

"If I dismount she might not let me get on again," I said miserably.

A little later the huntsman blew *drawn blank*, and brought hounds out of covert with the help of his whippers-in.

"Over to Lamport's kale now, sir?" he asked of the Master, who said: "That's right, Tom."

And now the trouble started. Martini had been expecting a thrilling run. When hounds moved off in the direction of the kale, she could hardly control herself. She trembled from head to foot, snorted and danced sideways, and then, quite suddenly, she broke into a gallop. She passed the second whipper-in, she passed the huntsman, and then the first whipper-in, who was leading the way to the kale, and she galloped down a grassy track into an open meadow. The wind was cold in my face; the sound of hound and horn still rang in my ears, mingled with the thudding of Martini's hoofs on the winter turf. I heard a man shout somewhere behind me. Was it a view halloa, or a message meant for me, I wondered. But I dared not look back. Ahead was another open gateway, leading on to a road. I felt sick with fear and my heart seemed to beat time with Martini's thudding hoofs. . . . Supposing we collided with a bus? . . . I should be killed. . . . There would be no escape. . . . I must stop. . . . I must stop, I thought. I lifted one hand from the lathered brown neck and took a tug at the reins. Martini seemed to increase her speed, though a moment ago I had thought that she could go no faster, and we sped through the open gate on to the road. And now the clattering of her hoofs drowned all other noise. We seemed alone, galloping to our doom in a silent world. If I had been born braver I would have flung myself to the ground. If I had been born with more brains I would have forced Martini into one of the hedges that sheltered the little country road from the wild winter winds and the hot sun of summer. But, being weak and afraid, I did neither. I sat very still, resting my hands on her neck, and prayed that she might stop, and prayed in vain. We galloped downhill and uphill and through a straggling village, where two small children ran shrieking to their mothers, and then we swerved left into a lane. Presently, I started to feel that I would fall off through sheer weariness. My knees felt that they would grip the saddle no more; my back felt tired and my fingers ached from pressing so hard on Martini's neck. And then a miraculous thing happened. Round the corner came a farm wagon and shire horse, led by a labourer, and the wagon was so wide that it took up all the lane and blocked the way. I had never before felt so grateful for anything as I felt for that wagon. I wanted to cry out, *thank you, thank you,* but I controlled myself and just gave a little shriek to let the labourer know that I was in distress. And then, to my great relief, Martini slowed up and stopped.

" 'Ounds 'ave crossed the main road a few minutes gone, miss," said the labourer helpfully.

"I didn't want the hunt," I gasped. "I want to go home. Do you know the way to Bannisters Farm, please?"

"You've got your pony in a muck sweat, 'aven't you?"

I dismounted, saying: "Yes, and I want to take her back. She's young and over excited."

The labourer scratched his head and remembered the way to Bannisters Farm, and presently I was leading my pony along the road to home, with a heavy heart and aching legs.

I had a long, cold walk in front of me and I felt tired and miserable, and wished that I had Tessa's energy and strength. Martini seemed to feel tired, too, and she dawdled and lagged, until my arms hurt from having to pull at her.

I wondered what my parents would say when they heard my sad story. No doubt they would both be bitterly disappointed. They wanted me to be dashing and brave. They wanted me to possess those qualities that they did not possess themselves.

It's not my fault I'm afraid and fragile, I was born that way, I decided. And, after all, they shouldn't be very annoyed, because they can't expect everything and I am good at dancing and sewing, and keeping my hands clean and my hair tidy.

With these thoughts I consoled myself as I trudged the last two miles along the winding country road to Bannisters Farm. The sun was out, thawing the grass and the hedges and lighting the clear cold sky; the wind had lost its sharpness and the air had a wonderful fresh quality, that should have cheered my heart. Everyone I met was smiling; the cows in the wet, sunlit meadows and the dogs and cats at the roadside and in the cottage gardens were happy. I was ashamed that I was miserable and I wished desperately that my parents had never bought Martini, that they had allowed me to continue to ride sweet, dear Rex, who is so kind and gentle.

CHAPTER TEN

"I BLAME that Guy Beaumont; he must have known the pony was a bolter. Fancy selling a dangerous animal to a little girl," said Mummy indignantly.

"Well, I'm going to put an advertisement in the paper right away," said Daddy. "The pony's not safe."

It was tea-time and I had told my parents all. And they had rung up Miss Stallwood, who had said: "Sell the animal. She's not fit for a child. I knew that as soon as I saw her the first time." And so I found that my parents were not cross after all, but quite sympathetic, and I felt less miserable and ate a large tea, for my long walk had given me an unusually large appetite.

"Never mind, Pippie," said Mummy. "We'll find you another pony with better manners, won't we, Daddy?"

Even George had been sympathetic. "The mare wants a man on 'er. She's too lively like for a girl," he had said, and it was his words that had given me courage to confess to my parents.

I slept long and well that night. My worries were over. I would never have to ride Martini again. My fears had come true. She was a bolter, a dangerous pony, but luckily she had not hurt me. She had been found out before she did any irreparable damage. I would never ride anything unsafe again. I had learned my lesson. I wakened with a light heart and an easy mind, and left George to groom Martini.

Four-year-old brown mare. 14.2 hands. By Rascal of Rapallo. Very quiet to handle. Good-looking and sweet-tempered. Jumps well and has been hunted. Keen.

The paper came out on Saturday. On Sunday morning a likely buyer came to Bannisters Farm. He was a dealer, a big fat man with a mackintosh without a belt and a homburg hat. He inspected Martini very carefully in the stable, feeling her legs, looking at her teeth and pushing her suddenly to test her wind.

Eventually he said: "Well, let's have a saddle on her. I would like to see the pony ridden."

My heart sank, my knees knocked and I felt faintly sick. I looked imploringly at Mummy, who said: "I'm afraid there's nobody to ride her, Mr. Hawkins, unless you ride yourself."

"No, I haven't been across a saddle since I put my knee out fifteen years ago," he replied.

"You see, we are selling Martini because she is too much for my daughter. She's too keen for Pip. She'd be all right with a stronger rider," said Daddy.

"Dear, dear, dear. Now what shall we do? Tell you what: I'll give you thirty-five for the pony," said Mr. Hawkins.

Mummy gave a gasp of indignation, but Daddy kept calm. "We are not going to accept anything like that. We gave a hundred for her and we don't expect to lose much," he said firmly.

"Did you indeed! Did you now! That's a lot for a pony like that. Well, let's see her trotted anyway," said Mr. Hawkins.

George led Martini out of the loose-box. She had not been exercised since my unfortunate hunt over a week ago and she was very fresh. and she was so busy bucking that she hardly trotted at all.

"So you gave a hundred pounds for that pony! Well, well, well. Next time you want a decent, quiet pony at a reasonable price, for a kiddy, Mr. Cox, let me know,"

She was so busy bucking

said Mr. Hawkins. "You can put her back. I've seen enough," he said to George.

"You are not interested then?" said Daddy.

"She's a nice-looking pony But I couldn't give you more than forty pounds or so. You see, she needs schooling, and it's dashed hard to find people to do any schooling nowdays. I couldn't consider any sum like the one you suggest," said Mr. Hawkins.

"Well, that's that, then," replied Daddy. "I'm sure we will sell her very easily."

"I disagree with you there. It's the lively, green ponies which are so hard to get rid of, and there are plenty of them about. I go around the country and I know," said Mr. Hawkins, getting into his car. "Well, good-bye and good luck," he added, driving away.

"What a horrible, downright man," said Mummy.

"... thought I would let him beat me down," commented Daddy.

On Monday Lydia Pike rang up and asked if she could come and look at Martini in the afternoon. She was searching for a likely show jumper, not exceeding 14.2. Daddy said he thought Martini was just the pony for her, being a very promising jumper with well let-down hocks. And at half-past two Lydia arrived, with a large brown and black Alsatian called Rudolf. She was a tall, hefty girl with big hands and feet, full lips and cheeks and a determined chin. Her medium brown hair was encased in a stout net, and she wore rather a heavy tweed coat and jodhs and walking shoes.

She shook Daddy firmly by the hand, saying: "Good-afternoon, Mr. Cox," in a very loud voice, and then she spied Martini looking over the loose-box door. "Ah, there's the pony! Looks nervous; a bit narrow between the eyes," she shouted, striding across the yard.

I was a little annoyed, because Martini has a very broad forehead and was not unduly nervous.

"Not a bad sort, Mr. Cox," Lydia continued in the same self-assured tone of voice, as she gazed over the loose-box door. "But I bet she's a handful for your little girl, isn't she?"

"Well, she needs a strong rider and Pip is very slight. I was the same at her age," said Mummy.

"I shall want to have a ride on her, of course," said Lydia.

George saddled and bridled Martini and we all went out into the meadow. I was struck by Lydia's brisk, strid-ing walk. Martini stood nicely while mounted and looked very graceful, as she pranced away across the wintry grass.

"A very abrupt girl, and rather big. I shouldn't like her for a daughter," remarked Mummy.

"She seems to know what she is talking about," said Daddy.

"She'll grow coarse when she's older, I know that type, coarse, rough and brusque. She won't be popular," Mummy went on.

"I think she'll master the pony," said Daddy.

Martini went well and quietly, till she was asked to canter, and then she let fling. She kicked up her heels and bucked, and Lydia lost a stirrup. Mummy gasped, and George said: "She's hot," and then Martini zipped into a gallop, and I thought she would never stop. But Lydia regain her stirrup and sat down in the saddle, and pulled and jerked at the reins with all her strength, till presently Martini began to slow up.

"She's got pluck, that girl," said Daddy.

"Oh, Pip, I'm glad we are selling the pony. She's wicked," said Mummy.

Soon Martini was walking again and Lydia rode up to us.

"A nice-looking pony, but with no manners at all and not suitable for children. May I jump her?" she asked.

"Yes, there's a fence at the far end," Daddy said.

Martini jumped well, although she put on rather an alarming spurt after the fence, and Lydia looked pleased with herself.

"Well," she said, returning to us, "what's your price, Mr. Cox?"

"Ninety-five pounds," said Daddy rather hesitantly.

Lydia's shrewd hazel eyes looked him full in the face. "I don't pay fancy prices," she said.

There was a moment's silence before Daddy said: "It's less than I paid for her."

"Ninety-five is ridiculous for a pony that can only be ridden by experts. I mean, look at her just now. No child or beginner could have sat those bucks. It's different for me. I've never been off a horse since I was four years old. Fifty is the most anyone could be expected to pay for your pony, Mr. Cox," said Lydia, ignoring Daddy's last remark.

"It seems very funny, I must say, Miss Pike, to hear you say that when we paid a hundred for the pony," said Mummy.

"Well, you were done. And I'm not the sort of person to be done," said Lydia with great firmness.

"Fifty is your limit then, is it?" asked Daddy.

"Absolutely," said Lydia, dismounting.

"You want the pony to train as a jumper?" asked Mummy.

"I don't know, of course, you can't tell over just one potty fence like that whether an animal will be a jumper or not. I should wait and see how she got on. That is if I bought her. And at the minute we seem at loggerheads. Supposing you think it over, Mr. Cox? I'll give you a ring to-night."

"A very determined young woman," remarked Daddy when Lydia had left.

"What an abrupt manner. But still, she would stick on. I'm glad we are selling the pony. After the way she bucked to-day, I should be scared stiff for Pip to mount her," said Mummy.

"I suppose we shall have to lose a bit. The Pike girl's right, we were *done* by those Beaumont people," said Daddy.

"Rotten lot. Fancy selling a dangerous pony to a little girl like Pip," added Mummy.

When Lydia Pike rang up that evening my parents accepted her offer of fifty pounds. Two days later Martini left Bannisters Farm for ever.

I never found a pony to suit me as well as Rex, and a year later gave up riding altogether, after a nasty fall, which broke my nerve.

PART THREE
By Lydia Pike

CHAPTER ELEVEN

WHEN I had finished talking to Mr. Cox on the telephone on the Monday evening, I thought I had bought a bargain. Fifty pounds, of course, was a fairish sum, but the pony was a good-looker and good mover with plenty of quality. Her bucks and bad behaviour did not worry me much. I had heard that she was a handful out hunting, but Pip Cox, I decided, was a feeble, nervous kid and enough to spoil any pony. I liked then, as now, a spirited and well-bred animal. I did not think much of the name Martini, so I rechristened the pony Good Form, which sounded well with the names of my other horses—Top Hat, Clean Sweep and Champion.

My father owns a firm which transports horses and cattle, so it was easy enough to bring Good Form to Little Frenchwood, our small, quaint and inconvenient village, which is miles from anywhere.

Mother was at the sink washing up lunch and Dad was filling up returns for the Government when Good Form arrived. I was showing Veronica, the girl Dad employs to help me with the horses, how to clean tack properly.

Good Form dashed down the ramp of the horse-box with a snort and I noted again her excellent hocks and sound legs and feet.

Ted Walker, who had driven the lorry, said she was a nice, breedy little mare. Mother is not very interested in horses, though she likes to see me carrying off prizes at the shows, but Dad came out and said that Good Form looked as though she could go. We saddled and bridled her straight away and I put her through her paces, and Dad was impressed.

"I reckon that if you get Jimmy Browne to help you, like he has with the others, that mare will give everyone in the county a big surprise this summer. They won't know whether they are coming or going," he said.

I was looking forward to showing Good Form to Jimmy Browne on the morrow. He knows everything there is to know about horses. He's practically lived with them since he was two years old. I don't think there can be anyone quite as expert at making jumpers pick their feet up as Jimmy. No horse can fool him. Though most of his own animals are fairly heavily built, he has a good eye for a lightweight and I thought he would probably like Good Form. "Yes, I shall jump her all the summer. And then make a pretty penny when I sell her in the autumn," I said.

The next day dawned bright, fair and frosty. At half-past ten I was on the road that leads to Jimmy Browne's place, a small, rather untidy farm. Good Form was full of beans, as the saying goes, and shied constantly. But you expect that sort of behaviour from a lively pony on a cold morning, and I was not at all perturbed.

Jimmy Browne was in one of the stables, saddling a big bay gelding with a Roman nose, when I arrived.

"Come and look at what I've got, Jimmy," I shouted.

He came out, a small tough man, with a cheery, weatherbeaten face and large capable hands. He looked Good Form over in silence, walking round her, feeling her legs and inspecting her teeth.

"She looks a handy sort of mare. Trot her up and back, so we can see her move," he said presently.

I rode Good Form out and down the road a little way and back again.

"That's all right. Have you time to give her a gallop in my meadow?"

"Certainly," I said, feeling pleased because I knew from Jimmy's expression and behaviour that he liked my new pony.

I galloped Good Form round his twenty-acre meadow, and she covered the ground at a surprising speed, in fact I could barely slow her up at the corners.

When I finally returned to Jimmy, who had been watching from the gate, he said: "Good for you, Lydia. You've got an eye for a horse—there's no mistake about that. She's a grand little mover. What did you pay for her?"

I told him, and he said: "Fair enough, fair enough."

"She jumps well, like a stag in fact," I added.

"*That* wouldn't surprise me either, not with those big hocks and good long thighs. Let's see her, if you've time."

I was all too willing and we went into the large level paddock where Jimmy has his jumps. He was, at present, training a youngster for the local point-to-point, and so his fences were long with wings and set well apart.

I approached the brush fence first. It was black and about three feet six in height, and it sloped away from me.

"I should leg her on a bit," called Jimmy.

I kicked and she bounded forward. I kicked again— one, two, three—and we were over and galloping towards the rail. I couldn't collect her; she was too excited now, but she wasn't going her fastest, so when we reached the wings I kicked again—one, two, three—and, somehow, she managed to bound forward, and again we jumped clear.

Then I started to pull her up. It was difficult, but I'm a strong rider, and I tugged my hardest, and presently she stopped.

"Good enough," said Jimmy. "You'll be winning every children's jumping class in the country next year, and the year after you can point-to-point her, when you are seventeen. Like to try her over something a bit higher?"

"Yes, please."

Jimmy raised the rail to four feet. "Bet she clears it. Now don't forget to leg her on a bit. It's not like a show jump; you can do it with a bit of speed."

"Right."

I rode as before and we cleared the fence with a flourish.

"Well done," called Jimmy.

I felt that I had ridden well, that I would make Good Form into a champion. I dismounted and patted her dark brown neck, which was damp with sweat.

"She can jump, that's certain. Now, let's hear—where did you pick her up?"

I told my story.

"Of course it was obvious that Pip Cox was a pretty wet kid and very spoilt. A Mummy's darling, with curled hair and as nervous as could be. Children like her shouldn't be allowed to keep decent ponies; they only ruin them," I finished.

"Quite a fair price," mused Jimmy, "but still, she's worth it every time. You've got the makings of a really top-class jumper, Lydia, what will put Top Hat, Champion and Clean Sweep right in the shade."

"Do you think I can beat Bob Saunders and Susan Watts?" I asked, for they were my two most dangerous rivals. Again and again we had jumped off at local shows, and sometimes one of us would win and sometimes another. Bob had four or five ponies and Susan only one, Beechnut.

"If we work hard every blooming day, wet or fine, in March, I think you will. But nothing in this world is done without hard work," said Jimmy.

"I would like to put them right out of the money," I said. "They won a jolly sight too much last year and Bob got so pleased with himself. Dad's sick of them too."

"Well, you come up here as often as you like. You know you're always welcome," said Jimmy.

Presently I left for home. I trotted Good Form because it was cold and she was too excited to walk. And I saw myself winning rosette after rosette with her. I saw Bob and Susan being defeated by myself in numerous jumps-off. I thought of all the money and all the cups that I would win. . . . My name will be in the national papers, I decided. . . . *Miss Lydia Pike, well-known rider, won the Children's Open Jumping at the White City yesterday, clearing five feet three inches in the jump-off.*

86

Veronica was moping about doing nothing as usual when I reached home, so I left her to rub down Good Form and went indoors. Mother was washing tea towels in the sink and I told her of my adventures. She listened patiently, but without enthusiasm. Dad was out on a job with our best horse-box. So eventually I confided in Rudolf, who was plainly interested in my ambitions.

CHAPTER TWELVE

BEFORE I go any further, I think I had better explain that, although I was only just sixteen when I bought Good Form, I had left school some eighteen months before. I am not stupid and I was not stupid when I was at Fily High School, but I simply was not interested in school work. I was too interested in horses. In fact I started coping when I was twelve by purchasing a strong brown pony at a fair with my savings for eight pounds and selling it two days later to a friend at school—at least the friend's father paid for it—for fifteen pounds.

Dad pays for my ponies' keep, and he bought Top Hat, Champion and Clean Sweep for me. But it was the money that I had accumulated from prize winnings and horse-coping that bought Good Form. I hoped, as I think I have said earlier, to sell her at a good profit, so that I could afford to buy an open jumper.

I started her education seriously at the beginning of March. Dad told his men to repaint, repair and re-erect my set of show jumps in our paddock, and Jimmy Browne brought his out of storage too.

I was kept pretty busy, as you can imagine, with four ponies to keep fit and well exercised. Veronica only mucks out, cleans tack and does some strapping. She is really too slow to be much help and I won't let her try riding any of my animals, because she is far too feeble; she would spoil them at once.

However, on the third of March I was able to practise my ponies for the coming shows. I jumped Top Hat, who is black all over, first. The course is comprised of a brush fence with guard rails of three feet six, a five-barred gate of three feet four, a wall of three feet six, a stile of three feet, and triple bars of three feet six.

Top Hat was a devil. As soon as I rode him into the paddock he started to rear. Eventually Dad fetched a whip and chased him over the brush fence, and once we had started, Top Hat was better. I was wearing spurs and I used my legs hard and we simply hurtled round the course, clearing the gate and wall, but knocking the triple bars and stile with front feet.

"Take him back and do those two again. But hit him first. Let him know he's wrong," called Dad.

I hit Top Hat twice and he reared. He refused to approach the gate until Dad got behind him with the whip; then he bounded forward and cleared it, but knocked down the stile.

"Try again," called Dad.

For half an hour I tried to make Top Hat clear the stile and then I had to give him up.

"Take him round to Jimmy's place to-morrow. Old Jimmy'll soon make him pick his feet up," said Dad.

I gave Top Hat to Veronica and mounted Good Form, who seemed excited by the presence of the jumps. She broke out into a sweat and, when I cantered her round the paddock, she kept her eyes on the jumps and tugged at the reins. I was riding her in a twisted snaffle, drop nose-band and running martingale, but I had difficulty in preventing her from galloping.

Presently Dad called: "Come on, let's see her jump. I haven't got all day to hang around, you know."

"All right, I was just loosening her up," I replied.

I turned her round and rode at the brush fence. She cleared it with feet to spare, landing well out the other side, but she knocked the gate with her front legs and ran out at the wall. I pulled her up sharply, scolding her, and rode at the wall again. She stopped dead in front of it.

"Punish her. Don't let her get away with that sort of thing," called Dad, and I hit Good Form three times with my long jumping switch.

She plunged and bucked, but I swung her round and put her at the wall again, and this time she scrambled over.

We approached the gate, which was well winged. I felt her hesitating and used my legs she still hesitated so I backed them up with my switch—one, two, three hits—and we were over at full gallop. She galloped twice round the field before I could stop her and turn for the triple bars.

I could hear my father shouting: "Stop her, girl. Pull on those reins. Don't gallop all over the place."

I rode the last jump with determination. Again Good Form hesitated and again I used my switch, but this time something went wrong. She took off too early, about six feet in front of the first bar, and landed on the third bar and all but came down. I fell forward and banged my nose on her neck. It was a horrible feeling. She must have knocked her legs pretty hard, because she limped for a few moments afterwards. I dismounted and patted her.

"Oh, knocked herself, has she? Never mind, that'll teach her not to be so careless another time," said Dad, coming across the paddock.

"I wonder if she's ever jumped a triple before or any show jumps for that matter," I mused.

"Oh, well, if she hasn't, she'll soon learn. Up you get and put her over those bars again. You must finish top, and I bet she picks her legs up this time."

Good Form, however, had no intention of approaching the triple bars again. She bucked and plunged and ran backwards and pawed the ground. She snorted and she sneezed, and she tossed her head. I used my legs and my switch, but without avail. Presently Dad lost patience.

"Where's my whip? I'll learn her to play up," he said.

"No, Dad, I'd rather ask Jimmy's advice before you start driving her over," I said, and I dismounted and gave my reins to Veronica.

"You are not going to give in to her, are you?"

"No, I'm going to take her round to see Jimmy, with Top Hat, first thing to-morrow," I replied firmly.

"Are you stark, staring mad? If you don't master that pony now, you'll never master it," said Dad.

"She's upset. I'd rather ask Jimmy first," I said, mounting Clean Sweep.

"Well, I wash my hands of that pony then, that's all there is to it," said Dad furiously, leaving the paddock.

Clean Sweep jumped the course clear, and when I put the jumps up to four feet he only hit the stile. I struck his legs sharply six times with my switch, to show him that he had been in the wrong, and then he cleared the stile with ease.

I jumped Champion, who is a solid, sensible cob with a docked tail, in the afternoon. He was careless as usual, but I sharpened him up with the switch and then he jumped quite well.

The next day I took Good Form and Top Hat over to Jimmy's place. His paddock was chock-a-block with jumps, all set very closely together, and with large solid wings.

"Now, what's the trouble?" asked Jimmy.

I told him.

"Oh, ruffled up your Dad, have you? You mustn't do that," he said. Then he called to one of his farm men: "Fred, get my long whip and bring it here, will you. "We'll have Top Hat first," he added to me.

"What do you think I ought to jump?" I asked.

"He's been hitting, hasn't he? We'll just have him over the single bar a few times."

The single bar was made of heavy wood and rested on wooden pegs in two posts at about four feet. Jimmy took his long whip and stood beside the jump.

"All set," he said.

After a short fight with Top Hat I approached the bar. About eighteen feet away I used my legs—one, two, three —and we jumped the bar clear, but Jimmy swung out his whip and caught Top Hat a sharp blow on both his front legs.

"There, that'll make him jump bigger next time," he said. "Come on, over again."

Once more Top Hat jumped clear and once more Jimmy struck him in mid-air with the whip.

"He can still jump higher, you know. He nearly touched it that time. Over again, and this time I'll see he picks his feet up."

But Top Hat had decided that he had had enough and reared whenever I asked him to jump the bar, so eventually Jimmy had to get behind him with the whip—Dad had learned his tactics from Jimmy—and slash him over the quarters, whereat Top Hat sprang forward and cleared the bar easily.

"There! That pony can jump all right. He's just bone idle, that's all there is to it. Supposing you jump him round a course now?"

"Okay."

I had rather a job to get started. In fact Jimmy had to assist with his whip again, but I jumped the four feet course of seven jumps clear.

"Good, good. He's learned his lesson. Now let's have the little mare," said Jimmy. "Be best to put the course down a bit, seeing she's new to it."

"Can I jump her over something low first?" I asked.

I put her at a stile of about three feet and she knocked it down.

"Hallo, hallo, so she's careless too, is she?" said Jimmy.

"I'll try her again," I said.

"Hit her hard on the take-off, that'll make her jump," said Jimmy.

I did as I was told, but she crashed the stile and, on

91

landing, shot into a gallop. It was with difficulty that I pulled her up.

"Let me just get there with my whip," said Jimmy. "We know she can jump higher than that. We've seen her many a time, haven't we?"

The new attempt proved no more successful. She hit the stile and Jimmy managed to strike her on the legs with his whip.

"Right, try again. And this time hold her back till you are in the wings. Always take stiles slowly. They are tricky things, you know."

His advice was useless, because I could not make Good Form approach the jump slowly. She was thoroughly excited by now, and if I tried to make her stand or wait for a moment she pawed the ground wildly and ran backwards. I knocked the stile three more times and Jimmy made me jerk her in the mouth directly I landed and hit her legs, so that she knew I was displeased with her carelessness. Presently even he became exasperated by her stupidity.

"She'll never clear it as long as she's tearing like that. Come here and let's have a look at that martingale. Perhaps we can strap her down a bit tighter."

He inspected my tack. "Yes, we'll have the drop noseband a hole tighter and the martingale can come in a couple of holes," he said, making the necessary alterations.

Then he called Fred and suggested that I should try her over a long bar held by him and his farm-hand. I accepted the suggestion and rode with great determination. I was going to make the brute of a pony jump at all costs. It was nice to find that I could now hold her, and I approached the bar sideways at a slow canter. She took off too late, and Jimmy and Fred shot up the bar and gave her a good bang on the hind legs. The next time she jumped clear.

"That's taught her a lesson. Now try the stile again," said Jimmy.

She jumped the stile clear and I felt heartened.

"I'll do the course now," I said.

I felt very confident now that my martingale seemed so powerful. Like Top Hat she played the fool a bit at the start, but once we were on the move she jumped better. In fact she cleared everything except the triple bars, which was the last obstacle.

"Hit her on the legs. Pull her up sharp. Let her know it right away," shouted Jimmy as we landed.

I obeyed his instructions and Good Form plunged and bucked.

"You shouldn't be so careless, old girl," I said.

I put her at the triple bars again and she misjudged the take-off completely, although I held her back till the very last moment, and she carried the top bar several yards across the paddock with her front legs.

"Try again and hit her on the take-off," shouted Jimmy.

But, like Top Hat, Good Form no longer wished to approach any of the jumps, and eventually Jimmy had to use his whip behind her. One blow on the quarters sent her bounding forward. For a few seconds the triple loomed before us and I used my switch. She took off and with a whisk of her quarters managed to clear the jump.

"There you are! What did I say? A good hit on the take-off works wonders sometimes. She's green, you see, doesn't know anything, got to be learned. Better put her over it just once more," said Jimmy.

Another fight ensued. Good Form thought she had had enough, but this time I managed to master her without Jimmy's help. I approached the triple slowly with my reins in one hand and my switch ready. But when I used my legs three strides away she took me by surprise and, snatching the reins, dashed sideways and past the jump. I was very angry. I pulled Good Form up with a jerk and hit her three times. Running out was a bad habit that I must nip in the bud. She bucked, and tried to unseat me.

"Now then! Get on, you brute!" I shouted, and, swinging her round, I rode at the triple again.

This time I used my switch on the take-off and we jumped clear. She was very excited and it took me a couple of minutes to pull her back into a walk. She was lathered with sweat and the reins were horribly sticky.

"I should jump her in spurs. That's the solution," said Jimmy cheerfully. "Then you can keep her straight and safely put your reins in one hand to hit her on the take-off "

"Right. I will next time. Now I must go. I'll bring both these round to-morrow. Dad's sending one of the men along to take that cow of yours into market, so I might get a lift. Good-bye and thank you."

Both Top Hat and Good Form were perfect beasts on the way home. Neither of them would walk a step. They tossed their heads and jogged and sidled and generally played the fool. I had risen early that morning and I felt fed up. I was riding Good Form and I kicked and shouted at her, but without avail. She was just downright obstinate and Top Hat, jogging too, encouraged her.

"I've got a jolly good mind to take you both for a five-mile gallop and I shall certainly cut your corn," I told them.

And when I got home and Mum, who was mashing potatoes, asked how my ponies had behaved, I said: "Oh, they were just about as stupid as they could be," and walked out of the kitchen, slamming the door.

CHAPTER THIRTEEN

EVERY DAY, wet or fine, I rode Good Form, and at least four days a week I jumped her. I wanted to win first, second, third and fourth at the Stringwell Show in the Children's Open Jumping Class. Two years before I had won second and third with Clean Sweep and Top Hat, but Bob Saunders had carried the first prize of ten pounds and a cup, with his ill-mannered brute of a cob, Nobby Boy.

Good Form improved, though she could still be a beast to ride. Twice a week Jimmy helped me, rapping her hind legs with a pole and sometimes tapping her in mid-air with a whip. I began to put her over larger fences, four and four feet six high, and, as Jimmy said, she certainly could lift herself when she took the trouble. But often, particularly over triples, she was careless. I tried making her approach her fences very slowly and I tried letting her go her own pace, but with no avail. Jimmy felt maddened sometimes.

"She's got it all there. She's just too darned lazy to use herself. Let her know it on the take-off. Let the old switch do some work. That'll learn her," he would say. And often he was right. A good sharp hit on the take-off would make her jump clear; but not always. Occasionally she seemed to have taken a particular objection to an obstacle and it seemed that nothing we could do would make her clear it. But Jimmy was unconquerable. More than a match for any horse, he would not let me go home until we had defeated Good Form. Once it grew dark before she cleared the triple bars at four feet six. but always we won in the end.

"See," Jimmy would say. "Never give in. That's the

95

She certainly could lift herself when she took the trouble

secret of mastering horses." Of course I had many fights
with Good Form. She would become fed up after being
punished for carelessness, and buck and kick and run
backwards, and paw the ground impatiently with her
hoofs. She was like a spoilt child and hated to be corrected or disappointed. But Jimmy had only to approach
with the whip and she would give in and attempt the
jump again. Jimmy liked her; he said she was a mare
with spirit and would become one of the finest jumping
ponies in England.

He was training a horse himself for the Stringwell
Show, a big bay gelding of 16.3 h. h., called Captain. Captain had jumped well at the end of the last summer and
had won fifteen pounds in seconds and thirds at small
shows during a fortnight in September. I hoped very
much that Jimmy would win the Open and Novice jumping classes this year, because he is so often unlucky. It

seems mean that a man who works so hard and posses-
ses such skill in the managing of horses should not win
more often. But Jimmy, of course, never sees it in that
light. He loses with a smile and I have never known him
lodge a complaint, though on many occasions he has had
good reason to do so.

Towards the end of March I heard, through our
grocer's wife, that a small horse show and gymkhana was
being held before the Stringwell Show, on April 2nd, at
Furnly Green, a tiny out-of-the-way village in the heart
of the country. I told Jimmy and suggested that I might
enter my ponies if the classes were suitable.

"Be just the thing for your little mare," he said. "A
nice quiet little show to settle her down before Stringwell.
I should enter her on all accounts, shouldn't hesitate."

I wrote for a schedule and continued to practise Good
Form. She had never jumped a clear round over a course,
but we were jumping her over four feet and four feet six
mostly now, and as Jimmy said, the fences at Furnly
Green would certainly not be over three feet.

I told my parents that I was going to make a fortune
this year out of my four jumping ponies.

When the schedule arrived I was pleased to discover
that there was a jumping class for children of seventeen
years and under, on ponies not exceeding 14.2 hands in
height. The first prize was rather mingy, only a pound,
but you can't expect to win anything worth talking about
at petty little shows held miles away from anywhere, and
I was only entering Good Form for the sake of her gaining
experience.

There were a few gymkhana events, too, and I decided
to take Champion, who is quite an old hand at that sort
of thing, and pick up a few extra prizes. Jimmy said he
would take Captain for the Open Jumping.

Accordingly, on the afternoon of April 1st we gave our
animals an extra long and extra special practice. Jimmy
believes strongly in a dress rehearsal on the evening before
a show. We rode at his place over a stiff course of jumps.

97

D

"If we put them over something big now, the jumps at the show won't half look low and easy," said Jimmy.

He and Fred rapped my ponies for me before I attempted the course. Champion went well, but the other three were excited by the rapping and behaved very foolishly. In fact I nearly lost my temper with Top Hat, who was an absolute idiot and refused to approach the wall. Of course he had to give in in the end, but the fight had wasted time and it was dark by the time I had finished with Good Form, who put up a bucking and plunging display, but eventually cleared a five-foot gate with ease.

The day of the Furnly Green Horse Show and Gymkhana was fine and bright with spring sunshine. I rose at six because Veronica is not reliable and I couldn't trust her to groom my ponies on her own. They were all stabled, but I left her the mucking out to do, because after all that's what grooms are for.

Captain and my four ponies travelled over to the showground in two of Dad's horse-boxes. Good Form was restless and pawed the floor with each forefoot in turn, which was rather irritating.

As soon as we arrived I knew that the show was going to be a potty, badly-run affair. The ring-posts were crooked and each one seemed to lean in a different direction from its fellows. The jumps were flimsy-looking and set very close together. The bending poles, lying on a corner, were miserable, spindly bean-sticks. There were incredibly few spectators to be seen.

A showing class was in progress and about ten ill-mannered, ill-bred and ill-groomed ponies were dawdling round the ring, watched from the centre by two obviously incompetent judges and ridden by the feeblest children you could imagine.

The time was ten o'clock. My jumping class was scheduled to begin at eleven, so Jimmy suggested that I should start practising right away. Veronica helped me saddle and bridle Good Form. I was riding her in a jumping saddle with forward flaps and a twisted snaffle with

98

a drop nose-band and a good tight running martingale. I put on my spurs, fetched my whip and mounted.

Jimmy and Ted, the driver of my horse-box, held the practice jump—a stout bar about ten feet long. Good Form was upset by the journey and excited. As soon as she saw the bar she began to buck.

"Put her over it low first, until she settles down," said Jimmy, dropping his hand so that the bar was only about two feet from the ground. I used my switch and spurs, and Good Form bounded forward and, with a terrific leap, cleared the bar.

"She's jumping cleanly to-day all right, thanks to yesterday evening," observed Jimmy.

"She's got it all there—the power behind, I mean," I said.

I jumped her over the bar at two feet several times, and then Dad arrived and Jimmy raised it to about three feet and rapped her with it when she was in mid-air.

"That's the stuff to give them," said Dad appraisingly.

Later Good Form started another fight and refused to approach the bar, but Dad got behind her with Jimmy's whip and then she gave in.

By eleven o'clock I had practised all my four ponies and was waiting in the collecting ring on Top Hat. I was pleased to find that neither Susan Watts or Bob Saunders were present. In fact there were no familiar faces among my fellow-competitors. I heard my name being whispered around. . . .

"Have you seen, Lydia Pike's here? You know, she wins everywhere. Ooooh, isn't it awful? I haven't a chance now."

"Lydia Pike's brought her three ponies. She's practically a professional. We haven't a hope."

I smiled. It was nice to be well-known. Those who had not actually seen me performing knew my face from photographs in the papers. One little girl stole up to me and whispered: "Which is Clean Sweep? The one who's won sixty rosettes." She was obviously one of my many admirers. I sent her to Veronica, who was hovering at the ringside with Good Form and Clean Sweep.

I was the only competitor in the class with more than one pony, so I jumped first.

And Top Hat jumped well. The fences were very low, mostly under three feet, and, thanks to Jimmy's rapping, he cleared them all. It is true that he nearly jibed when he had to pass the entrance of the ring, but the sight of Jimmy approaching with a whip sent him forward again.

Faint applause and a voice through a crackly microphone announcing "A clear round" accompanied me from the ring. I handed Top Hat, who was lathered with sweat, to Veronica and mounted Good Form. She was trembling with excitement, trembling and tossing her head and prancing. A few of the more juvenile spectators gasped, "Ooh, isn't she lovely!" But, as she tugged at my arms, I felt irritated.

"Shut up, can't you," I said.

Presently my number was called and Jimmy led me into the ring. On my left I heard someone say, "There she goes on another pony. Don't say she's going to jump all four. It just isn't fair at a little gymkhana like this."

They are jealous, I thought. I trotted Good Form up to the far end and rode her slowly at the brush fence. She was nervous and hesitant, but when I used my spurs she bounded forward and we cleared the brush by feet.

The stile and gate that followed were easy, but Good Form was becoming more and more excited. It was all that I could do to hold her, and when she reached the entrance she tried to gallop me out of the ring. Luckily Jimmy was again ready with a whip, which he cracked in her face. She stopped, stood for a moment and then started running backwards. I used my spurs, but without effect. The show was not being judged under British Show Jumping Association Rules, and I wondered whether turning round would count as a fault. I was still in my mind debating this point when Jimmy shouted, "Get on, Get on," and, clicking his tongue, hit her from the far side of the ring ropes with his whip. She bounded forward and then stopped again and ran backwards. Then Jimmy did a very brave thing; he walked into the ring and led her past the entrance and, with a slash with the whip on her quarters, put her at the wall. She leaped forward, hesitated as she found herself between the wings, and then, feeling my spurs, jumped the wall, scattering a row of bricks. She was very excited by now and carelessly hit the next jump—a flimsy bar—and the triple.

Jimmy was waiting for me at the exit.

"Hit her across the legs now with your switch. Let her know she was wrong. It's the only way she will ever learn," he said.

I hit Good Form's back legs and scolded her, but Jimmy was not satisfied.

"Here, give her to me. She's got to be learned," he said, and, taking Good Form, he struck her six times across her legs and stomach with his whip. She reared and plunged, but he jerked her to a standstill. "She'll know to be more careful next time," he said.

Clean Sweep and Champion were the only two ponies to jump clear rounds besides Top Hat, and so I won first, second and third, and several of the local children were very annoyed.

"Look as though you've had a walk over," said Dad. "Pity the new little mare didn't jump better."

"Never you mind. She will win in time, you'll see," said Jimmy.

I won most of the competitions too, on Champion. In fact I think I came away with about eight rosettes.

Poor Jimmy was unlucky in the Open Jumping. Captain was an absolute brute when he had to pass the entrance and refused the wall twice, and so Jimmy only picked up a mouldy second of thirty bob.

After the show Good Form put up a surprising display and refused to be boxed. We had no end of a time with her. She reared and ran backwards, and kicked out at

Jimmy when he got behind her with his whip. Neither coaxing nor hitting would get her in.

She wouldn't let us pick up her front feet to place them on the ramp, in fact she struck at us whenever we put out a hand to touch them.

Eventually a very trying man, who believes himself an expert, came and helped us. He patted and talked to Good Form and then he lunged her round a few times on the end of a halter rope with Jimmy's whip. I thought he was barmy at first, but in the end he managed to get Good Form up the ramp and into the horse-box.

"We'll have to work hard. That mare will need a lot more schooling and rapping if she's to do any good at Stringwell," said Jimmy as we left the untidy little showground.

CHAPTER FOURTEEN

NO ONE can say that Jimmy and I did not work very hard on Good Form during the next three weeks. Every day, and sometimes twice a day, we gave her a lesson, and we did everything possible to make her careful about clearing obstacles. I jumped her in bandages with a little gorse put in between the cotton wool and the bandage, so that it pricked her legs if she was stupid enough to hit a jump with her cannon bones. Fred and Jimmy rapped her tirelessly, and I always pulled her up sharply, almost on the landing stride, if she knocked a fence, and hit her front legs with a switch.

Sometimes the weather was bad and the ground was greasy, and then we concentrated on the rapping with a single bar. Jimmy and Fred would each stand one end and when Good Form was in mid-air they would jerk the bar up so that it knocked her on the legs. As a result Good Form was always trying to jump higher and higher, which was excellent for her muscles and a good cure for carelessness.

She still had her stupid attacks of temperament now and then when Jimmy would have to fetch his long whip, and once she managed to get me off. She refused to approach the triple bars—our worst fights always occurred by the triple bars—and then started her usual running backwards, pawing the ground and bucking tricks. I was as safe as a house until Jimmy came along with his whip and then she took me by surprise. She reared and I leaned forward; she plunged and then quite suddenly she swung round, causing me to lose a stirrup; then she bucked, twisting in the air. In a few moments I was lying on the ground. Not badly hurt, of course, but a little shaken—it's not often a horse or pony puts me down. Jimmy caught Good Form and gave her a couple with the whip, just to show her that we were not going to stand any more of *that* kind of nonsense, and then I mounted again and after a little trouble made her jump the triple bars, which were four feet three. That was the one and only time that Good Form had me off and she was no easy ride, I can tell you.

Clean Sweep, Champion and Top Hat were all jumping well, though napping a little now and again. I took them to two or three shows between Furnly Green and String-well and won a few prizes—about fifteen pounds worth, I should say, which wasn't bad considering they were pretty potty shows with mingy prizes.

Good Form, though, I was holding back as a surprise for Stringwell. She had more jump in her than my other ponies, and when she made up her mind she could clear five feet easily. I wanted to amaze all my rivals with her, to shatter their hopes. I wanted to win at all the big shows, at the Royal Counties and the White City. I wanted to bring her out like a bombshell.

And at last the day came, the day of the Stringwell Show. I wakened confident, with high hopes. The evening before, Good Form had jumped brilliantly and without a quarrel. She had managed to clear the triple first try at four feet six and, having replaced the twisted snaffle with a curb, I could control her easily. Dad was optimistic too.

"If only you can keep her steady, you'll be all right," he said.

And Mum, watching me eating my breakfast of bacon and eggs, said: "Well, are you going to do your stuff to-day and bring back ten pounds?"

"I hope to bring back twenty—first, second and third," I replied with a laugh as I thought of Bob and Susan's surprise.

"I think Top Hat is going to do the best. He's got such a funny little glint in his eye, he really has," said Veronica as we gave the ponies a quick brush.

"You're wrong as usual," I told her. "It's Good Form's turn to-day. She's going to sweep the board. She's got more scope and more power than any pony we've ever had in these stables."

The day was wild and windy, and dark high-flying clouds threatened rain. It is in this sort of weather that horses so often play the fool, but I never suspected that Good Form might be affected by it.

When I arrived, Dad, who had travelled over by car, suggested that I might look at the cups, which were by the secretary's tent.

"They are really lovely," he said. "There's a great big silver one for the Children's Jumping—look well on our mantelpiece—and another bigger one for old Jimmy—can't be worth less than fifty pound."

"Oh, I *must* win to-day. I simply must," I said, gazing a few moments later at the prizes.

"Well, it's now or never. You'll be too old next year," said Dad.

On our way back to the horse-box I met Bob Saunders.

"Hallo. Got a fresh one here to-day, haven't you?" he asked.

"How do you know?" I felt irritated.

"Friend of mine saw it at Furnly Green," said Bob.

"She's improved a lot since then," I said.

"Wouldn't know her for the same mare now," added Dad.

"Ah, well. I've got four here too. Don't know how they'll go, though. If they jump to-day like they did last night, they'll not win a single ribbon."

"Bad as that, is it?" said Dad. "We must be getting on. See you later."

Presently I was putting my ponies over the practice jump. Good Form was even more excited than she had been at Furnly Green. It was only with the greatest difficulty that I could make her approach the bar slowly. As soon as I turned her towards it, she wanted to gallop, and if I asked her to wait for a moment she bucked and ran backwards and plunged. Each time she managed to get away from me too early—I like to let my ponies go about three strides from the take-off—and then she generally hit the jump. It was really very irritating, particularly as Bob Saunders and Susan Watts were watching, and I nearly lost my temper with her.

My other ponies did not jump very well either. Champion was careless. Clean Sweep was hesitant and tried to cat-jump, and Top Hat was very excited and inclined to rear.

Dad put their behaviour down to the wind. "They'll be all right when they are in the ring. They're just playing you up," he said.

But Mum was not so optimistic. "Doesn't look as though you are going to win anything to-day, Lydia. I suppose that Susan Watts and the Saunders boy will take home everything as usual," she said in disgruntled accents.

"Don't be downhearted. Never pays. A merry heart goes all the way," said Jimmy without much conviction.

A little later competitors for the Children's Jumping Competition were called to the collecting ring, and I talked to Susan Watts, who was looking every bit as pale and frightened as usual.

"I expect you will win to-day," she said. "I feel awful and poor little Beechnut is trembling all over with nerves. Don't you feel terribly miserable?"

"No," I answered firmly. "I wouldn't come to shows if they made me feel miserable. Good-bye. I must keep Top Hat on the move or he might nap."

"Oh, darling Beechnut never naps," said Susan.

The course was a large one with the jumps set in a figure of eight. The triple, perhaps, was the most formidable. The fifth obstacle, it was directly away from the collecting ring and about four feet in height with a spread of roughly five feet.

"You'll have to be careful with all of them there. Use your spurs, sharpen them up as you pass the entrance," said Jimmy.

Bob Saunders was the first to jump the course. He made a clear round on Nobby Boy, a brown cob with a docked tail. Then it was my turn, and Top Hat bucketed all the way up to the start. He cleared the first four fences magnificently, but as we passed the entrance he took me by surprise and stopped dead. I used my switch and my spurs at once, but he only reared. I looked at Jimmy, who was standing at the ringside, in the hope that he might help me, but, as the jumping was being judged under British Show Jumping Association Rules, he dared not do more than click his tongue and make low growling noises. I had never known Top Hat so obstinate before; he simply would not go forward, and I couldn't turn him round because that would have made a fault. The crowd at the ringside made ridiculous remarks and some idiotic boy yelled: "Ride him, cowboy." Dad said: "Give him the switch, girl." I hit Top Hat again and again, but each time I hit him he reared. Suddenly a judge blew his whistle and a steward told me that I had exceeded the time limit.

I was furious and so was Jimmy. As soon as I was out of the ring, I dismounted and hit Top Hat six times on

106

the poll to show him that he must not rear. Then it was time for me to ride Champion. Bob had just jumped another round, making two faults with his black mare, Magic, and I felt grim with determination as I entered the ring for the second time.

Champion seemed quiet and sedate after Top Hat, but he cleared the first four jumps well. It was the triple that he hit with forelegs and I don't know why. I certainly used my legs hard enough. The other three jumps he cleared well. Susan and Beechnut were the next to compete; they made two faults, refusing at the double gates.

Then a scruffy girl on a bay pony attempted the course and was disqualified with three refusals. It was my turn again, and Clean Sweep made a mess of things by knocking down three fences with his forelegs and refusing the triple twice.

So now I had my only chance of winning with Good Form. And when, the last to compete in the class, I entered the ring I saw the silver cup in my mind's eye and thought of the ten pounds. Mum had said: "Are you going to do your stuff?" and Dad: "Now or never. You'll be too old next year." I must win. I simply *must*, I thought, as I rode to the start, and before I put Good Form at the first fence—a brush—I leaned down and tapped her legs with my switch.

"Now be careful," I warned. She sprang forward with her ears back and we sailed the brush, and we were approaching the gate too fast for safety. I pulled on the reins in an attempt to steady her, but she only increased her speed. We crashed the gate, and on landing she put on a spurt, so that, in spite of my frantic pulls, we were approaching the wall at a fast gallop. I tugged and tugged but all in vain; we knocked the bricks off the wall, increased again and crashed the parallel bars. Now the entrance to the ring was opposite us, before the turn for the triple, and Good Form paid no attention to my pulls on the reins. I saw Jimmy with his big whip run and stand there blocking our way. I pulled again and Good

He made a clear round

Form saw him too, and hesitated, causing my hopes to rise.
I wrenched at her mouth and she turned, but not for the
wall as was my intention. She was panicking now. She
snatched at the bit, leapt the ring ropes and two rows of
empty chairs, and galloped away across the show ground
like a mad thing. I heard Dad shout. A screaming mother
dragged her tot from my path. A string of youths shouted,
"Hi, look out," and fled to the shelter of a beer tent. A
group of horse-box men yelled: "Whoa, steady there,
steady." A car swerved out of my way. I felt furious ....
I was making a fool of myself. I guessed that Bob and
Susan would be laughing at me. Angrily, I tugged at the
reins, saying: "Whoa, you little fool."

The man at the microphone announced that Mr.
Robert Saunders had won the Children's Jumping with
Miss Susan Watts second. I could not hear who was third,
but I guessed it to be Bob. Suddenly I felt even more
furious. I jerked and wrenched, and jerked and wrenched
at Good Form's mouth, shouting: "Whoa, you brute,
whoa!" I hate an animal to make a fool of me and, looking back, I think those moments were some of the most
irritating of my life. And then suddenly for no reason at
all she stopped. In that instant my feeling of annoyance
turned to one of real rage. I suppose I saw red, as the
saying goes, and, dismounting, I struck Good Form across
the face with my switch. She threw up her head and
sprang away from me, jerking my arm which held the
reins. Her wild eyes and heaving flanks infuriated me. My
arm hurt. I heard the crowd clapping as the winners of
the Children's Jumping left the ring. How could I face
Bob and Susan and my parents? That silly little fool
Veronica would yatter away if I went back to the horse-
box. Oh, how I hated Good Form! I turned round and
struck her across the stomach and on the flanks.
Goodness knows she needed it.

And then a voice behind me said: "Steady there,
young lady—none of that. It wasn't the pony's fault."

It was a young farmer who had spoken. Why he should

profess to know anything about horseflesh, I can't think. I had certainly never seen him at a horse show before.

"There's no need to interfere. This is my business. The pony needs to learn a lesson," I retorted, walking away with Good Form. I nearly ran into Susan a moment later.

"Hard luck. That little mare is very excitable, isn't she?" said Susan, and I fancied I saw a pleased smile belying her words. Inside she was laughing at me of course, thinking I had made a fool of myself.

"She's not excitable. She's just jolly obstinate. She needs to learn to do as she's told," I replied, hastening on my way.

My parents were standing by the beer tent.

Mum said: "Well, you've made a proper mess of things today, Lydia. You had better sell that pony before she makes a fool of you again. Goodness alone knows she can't be worth much. She's like a mad thing."

"Don't know why you were ever fool enough to buy her," said Dad.

"Oh, shut up," I said. "You've made mistakes yourself. I'm going to see Jimmy."

CHAPTER FIFTEEN

ONCE I have decided to sell a pony I get rid of it as quickly as possible. It was obvious that Good Form had not the right temperament for a show jumper, so she was useless to me, and I sent an advertisement to *Horse and Hound* and the local paper on returning from the show. I did not quote a price, but I decided to ask sixty guineas. I had put a lot of work into Good Form and I more than deserved a ten guinea profit. The same night I rang up several local horse-dealers who are acquaintances of mine, and told them that I had a keen, good-looking half-bred pony mare for sale which couldn't quite make the grade for show jumping, but was fast, tireless and sound.

Then I sat back and waited, and at the end of a week I received two replies to my advertisement in *Horse and Hound*. One from a Mrs. Rushwood, of Stanley Court, Speedwell, who wanted a gymkhana pony for her eleven-year-old daughter, who was a grand little horsewoman. The other from a Lettie Lonsdale, who merely asked for full particulars, and lived eight miles away.

I wrote immediately to Mrs. Rushwood explaining that Good Form was very quick on her feet, fast and handy, and would make a tip-top gymkhana pony in a very short time. And I rang up Lettie Lonsdale and suggested that she should come and see Good Form. She agreed to come with her parents on the following day, but said that she was afraid they could not afford to pay much for a pony and were really looking for a cheap rogue. I said Good Form was worth more than the amount that I was asking for her, and as Lettie Lonsdale seemed shy of knowing the real price I said goodbye and rang off.

I rose early next day and rode Good Form for two hours in the early morning. She was very fresh and I wanted to tire her, so I galloped her round and round our largest field till she was dripping with sweat. Veronica groomed her while I was having breakfast, and by the time the Lonsdales arrived she looked as though she had not been ridden that morning at all.

Mr. Lonsdale looked like an awful cross schoolmaster. He peered through horn-rimmed glasses. He stooped and his hair was too long and his clothes old and worn. Mrs. Lonsdale was small and light with untidy mouse-coloured hair. Her manner was affected; she gesticulated with her hands and was obviously insincere. She was most unsuitably dressed in corduroy trousers and sandals, and a polo-collared pullover. Lettie was tall for her age—she was thirteen—with green eyes and her mother's hair. Her legs were thin. She did not look strong or tough enough to be a good rider.

They had two enormous bloodhounds—ugly animals, I think—with them.

"Now I had better tell you straight away. None of us know anything about horses," said Mrs. Lonsdale. "Lettie has ridden for quite a long time, and she jumps and hunts and does some gymkhanas, but she's completely ignorant about splints and spavins and herring guts—or whatever it's called. David, my husband, is utterly useless as far as animals are concerned; he literally hasn't a clue. And I've only gleaned a few bits and pieces from looking after Pablo, our present pony, who's really more like a large dog. So we are really completely at your mercy."

"Well, here's the pony, anyway," I said, leading the way to Good Form's loose-box.

Of course, I thought, the Lonsdales are quite mad. Why didn't they bring someone who *does* know something about horses to advise them? They really deserve to be done.

"Oh, isn't she lovely. I love her colour. She's got nice short cannon bones and nice long forearms," said Lettie.

"She's adorable and so delicately made," said Mrs. Lonsdale. "Come and look, David."

Mr. Lonsdale, who had been hovering dejectedly in the background, now came forward and peered over the stable door.

"Yes, he's a very handsome creature," said Mr. Lonsdale.

"She's a mare," I said. "Veronica, will you put on her tack? The double bridle. Then I'll let them see her ridden."

A few moments later I was cantering Good Form round the field. Thanks to her earlier exercise, she was quiet and, in a double bridle, easy to stop. I kept on the outside of the field, away from the jumps, which would have excited her.

"She's terribly graceful," said Mrs. Lonsdale.

"Can I have a ride on her now? Do you always ride her in a double bridle?" asked Lettie.

"Yes, here you are," I said, dismounting. "No, sometimes I ride her in a snaffle."

"I noticed at Stringwell that you were jumping her in a curb, drop nose-band and running martingale," said Lettie, and I realised that she was not so foolish as she had seemed.

"Show jumping, of course, is a bit different. You've got to have such perfect control or you can't judge the strides and take-offs right," I said.

Lettie rode away on a loose rein. She sat too far forward in the saddle, with her legs too far back. I felt annoyed that she had seen me at Stringwell Show. I turned to Mrs. Lonsdale.

"Your daughter rides with her legs too far back and she sits too far forward in the saddle," I said.

"Oh, but Lettie believes in the Continental seat. She's really terribly keen on it," said Mrs. Lonsdale.

"I don't know why anybody should want to imitate foreigners. Everyone knows that the English are the best riders in the world. I was practically born in the saddle," I told her.

"Really? Now that's most frightfully interesting. Did you start on one of those tiny Shetlands with a basket saddle? I think they are simply marvellous."

"Rather inconvenient to be *born* in a saddle," said Mr. Lonsdale.

"Oh, look at the pony now. What do you call her? Isn't she lovely?" said Mrs. Lonsdale.

"Lettie tells me he jumped out of the ring in the middle of a performance at some show or other," said Mr. Lonsdale.

"She's a mare," I said.

"But did she really jump out of a ring, over the ropes and chairs and everything?" asked Mrs. Lonsdale.

"She got over-excited, but she won't do it again," I said.

"He must be quite an individual," said Mr. Lonsdale.

"Not *he*, darling, *she*. It's a mare," said Mrs. Lonsdale.

"She's by Rascal of Rapallo, and she's an excellent hunter with lovely manners and quite tireless. I doubt that you could find a better pony anywhere—not for the price, anyway," I said.

"Where did you get her from? Did you break her yourself, or was she broken?" asked Mrs. Lonsdale.

"I bought her from a very nervous girl who couldn't manage her and lives by Longhatch, at a farm."

"Not Pip Cox? You don't mean to say this is her pony. Well, how extraordinary! I must tell Lettie," cried Mrs. Lonsdale.

"Good Form's improved a lot since she left Bannisters Farm," I told them.

"Yes, I remember Pip," said Lettie, on hearing the news. "She gave some wonderful display in the hunting field, galloped away into the distance or something, and created quite a stir. So this is Martini."

I was becoming angry. These Lonsdales were deceptive. They knew too much. They would never buy the pony now.

"Have you finished trying her yet?" I asked.

"Can I just put her over the triple or something?" asked Lettie.

"Yes," I said. "Anything."

"Why did you change her name? I think Martini is so lovely," asked Mrs. Lonsdale.

"Not suitable for a show jumper," I said.

"Did you mean to make her into a jumper then?" asked Lettie.

"I considered it."

Good Form refused the triple bars twice, plunged and bucked, and then, to my surprise, jumped it.

"Jolly good, Lettie," shouted Mrs. Lonsdale.

"She would make a show jumper. I'm sure she would,

she's got such scope, and she gives you such a marvellous feeling of power," said Lettie.

"I'm not having you turning into one of those dreadful children who go round all the shows collecting cups," said Mr. Lonsdale.

"I think you've tried her enough now, haven't you, Lettie? We can't use up too much of Miss Pike's time," said his wife.

"Sorry. Yes. I have finished. Thank you very much."

I had given up hope now and I hurried them back to the stable. They were a queer family, quite unconventional, I decided, watching them return to their car with the two bloodhounds, Jasper and Justice.

"Oh, look at all the other ponies!" cried Lettie, seeing the row of loose-boxes round the corner.

"I think you are wonderful, having and schooling so many all by yourself," said Mrs. Lonsdale.

"You told me a thousand times not to forget my cheque book, but you haven't asked the price of the pony yet, Janet," said Mr. Lonsdale.

"What are you asking for her, Miss Pike?" asked Mrs. Lonsdale, suddenly becoming brisk and business-like.

"Sixty."

"Oh, dear," said Lettie.

"You won't come down, I suppose?" said Mrs. Lonsdale dubiously.

"No, she's a good pony and worth every bit of that."

"We can't by any chance get up to that, can we, David?" she asked, looking at her husband.

"No, we must find something costing less, I'm afraid. Sorry, Lettie."

They got into the car.

"Thank you so much," said Lettie. "If you ever want to sell her for less you will let us know, won't you?"

"Of course."

"Goodbye, Miss Pike, and thank you so much." called Mrs. Lonsdale.

They backed the battered car down the drive and, waving, disappeared from my view.

I thought: That's over. The child would never have managed Good Form anyway. I expect I'll sell the pony quite easily. Pity I haven't ridden her in more gymkhana events. Every day she stays here she's costing me money.

Indoors, Mother was getting tea. "Well, did you sell the animal?" she asked.

"No, they wouldn't pay the price."

"I'm not letting you keep that pony here, eating its head off and bringing in nothing. You'll have to take less, that's all. You should never have bought her," said Dad.

"Send her to the next sale," said Mum.

And that, to cut a long story short, is what I did. Mrs. Rushwood did not write again.

On a wet May day I plaited her mane, pushed her head into my cheapest and most disreputable halter and sent her to Stringwell Market, where the quarterly Horse Sale was being held. Dad wouldn't let me put a reserve on her so she went for thirty-two quineas to, of all people, Lettie Lonsdale.

What could be more infuriating? I'm sure the Lonsdales would have paid fifty, if I had asked them. But there it is . . . Horse-dealing is like that, and you have to learn to take the rough with the smooth. Good Form was a horrible brute; she hadn't the right temperament for a show jumper and I was glad to be rid of her.

A few weeks later I bought a nice little blood horse of fifteen two, which I am sure will make a topping jumper. I have called him Top Notch.

PART FOUR
By Lettie Lonsdale

CHAPTER SIXTEEN

WE LIVE in Cherryford, an old village with an old bridge that crosses the shallow waters of the river Lynne; a village, unfound by townsmen or modern house-builders, of low-roofed cottages and dreaming houses and quiet sheltered gardens; a long low village of trees and mossy walls, and cobbled yards.

Our house stands on the left bank of the Lynne, and all day and night we can hear the murmur of the water amongst the rushes. And in the summer when we take tea in the garden two stately swans drift by our lawn and beg for food. We have christened them the Lady of Shalott and Sir Lancelot.

Our house is a shabby pink—badly painted because Mummy and I were the painters. The outside woodwork is an unusual colour; it is neither light nor dark and resembles Picasso's blue.

By the back door there are two pink loose-boxes, standing in a small cobbled yard that is rough and uneven and difficult to sweep. A white five-barred gate leads from the yard to a little crooked orchard, fenced by green hedges, which are kind to the eyes and harbour the birds in spring.

To Cherryford I brought Martini in the dusk, when the Lynne's waters were darker than the darkening skies, and the river meadows drifting into slumber.

I had ridden her from Stringwell Market, bareback in a plain snaffle, and I already loved her long stride and gay carriage. She had shied and jogged in the town, but out in the open country she had become calm, as though quietened by the stillness of the evening, and had walked on a loose rein.

Our village is very interested in the movements and behaviour of its inhabitants. Nothing goes unnoticed. As I rode down the old and lovely street, people came to their windows and doors to watch me on my way.

Tatters, my wire-haired terrier, was waiting for me in the yard. He's a disreputable character, always rabbiting and tearing his ears, and getting stuck in holes. But he is very brave and very sporting. One winter he killed a fox after a terrific battle in an earth in Duke's Wood.

He's fond of horses and I was glad to see that he took a liking to Martini.

Mummy came running out of the back door. "Here you are at last! We wondered if you were ever going to get here. Push her into the loose-box. Nick and I have put some hay and water ready. And then come in and have some supper. There's ham and salad and cider."

At that moment my seven-year-old brother, Nicholas, came through the window.

"She looks jolly good. I expect Pablo will be pleased. Why did you ride her without a saddle?" he asked.

"Because Pablo's wouldn't fit her," I said.

"Why wouldn't it fit her?" asked Nicholas.

"Because it is too small."

"Why's it too small?"

Oh, do stop asking questions. Why are your old clothes too small for me? Because I'm larger than you, being older," I said, feeling exasperated.

"Is Marty older than Pablo? And will Pablo grow bigger like me?" asked Nicholas.

"No. Now do stop. I want to settle Martini," I told him.

"When are you going to introduce Pablo to her?" he asked.

"To-morrow."

"Why not now?"

"Because I'm not."

"Why's she sleeping in the stable? It's so hot."

"Because she's been in since the autumn."

"In where?"

"A stable."

"Which stable?"

"Pip's and Miss Pike's stables."

"Who's Miss Pike?"

"You know perfectly well, Nicholas. We've been talking about Miss Pike for days."

"*I've* never heard you."

"That's because you never listen to what people are saying."

"I do."

"You know, it's your bed-time," I said hopefully.

"No, it's not. Mummy said I could stay up ever, ever so late to-night."

"All right. Let's go in to supper now," I suggested, giving Martini a last pat.

"You've forgotten to say good-night to Pablo."

"No. I haven't. I'll do it later when I shut up the hens."

Indoors we all talked about Martini. At least Mummy and I talked and Nicholas asked questions and Daddy listened.

Riding back from Stringwell I had laid my plans. I knew that Lydia Pike's rough handling had made Martini frightened of her mouth, constricted and excitable. I would start to cure these faults by hacking her quietly in a snaffle on a loose rein.

It was term-time and I had to go to school every week-day, but my prep. was not difficult and I could spare an hour for riding in the long summer evenings.

"If you get into real difficulties you can write to Pierre," said Daddy.

I think I must explain now that Monsieur Pierre de St. Denis, the well-known French horseman, is a friend of my father. Last summer he asked my parents and I to stay at his estate on the outskirts of Fontainbleau. He lent me a little grey mare, called Chiffon, to ride, and instructed me in the art of equitation. It is from him and the books he recommended me to read that I have learned most about riding and schooling. And I shall never forget those six wonderful weeks in France.

After supper I paid a call on Martini and then wandered out into the orchard to say good-night to Pablo, the little black pony on which I first started to ride. He was lying against the hedge in a corner, looking very snug and sweet. The night was cool and clear. The moon sailed high, amongst her stars, touching the cherry boughs with silver and casting great pools of silver by the gate. I could see the Lynne, drifting before the breeze with barely a ripple. I could see the noble outline of Martin's heard above the loose-box door.

"Pablo," I said, "one day I'm going to be a famous equitation expert. I'm going to jump for England, in Dublin, in Nice, in Rome, in New York, all over the world."

I put an arm round the little black neck and looked at the moon and stars, so clear and lovely in the evening sky. I wished that I could express my feelings in oil on canvas. The pools of silver and darkness . . . the cherry boughs . . . the dead elm, sharp and naked, etched against the sky . . . the stillness and the winding river . . . the old pink house silent amongst the trees . . . the stable roof . . . the curving lawn . . . the sleeping flowers. The beauty of it almost hurt me. My ambitions faded. I patted Pablo and then wandered slowly into bed.

CHAPTER SEVENTEEN

I GAVE Martini one day in which to settle down and then I started schooling her in earnest.

At half-past four each day I would return from school, gobble my tea, do my prep, and then ride till darkness. The weather was perfect; the evenings warm and fine. Those last hours before nightfall always passed too quickly. My efforts were well rewarded. Each day Martini seemed quieter and more confident. She shied less often; she became steadier on the bit; she learned to trot on a loose rein. But I vowed not to canter her for a fortnight. I wanted the rides to be as peaceful and calming as possible. Often I would stop and, dismounting, let her graze while I admired the sunset . . . golden sands and rocks red-tipped and a darkening sea of blue.

Sometimes when we turned for home all the world seemed asleep. Dusk had fallen and the birds' last songs had faded. The wild flowers in the woods and at the roadside were shut in slumber. The fields lay silent in the gathering darkness. The trees loomed dark and eerie, watchful sentinels of the night. Far away beyond the river an evening star was shining and a great stillness descended on the land.

Presently May turned to June and all Cherryford was bright with apple blossom and sweet with the scent of hay. Old Bob Silver, the boatman, did some trade with his boats and Nicholas started to learn to swim.

I cantered Martini during the first week-end, and a few days later I started to school her in a corner of the orchard. I was dissapointed to find that balancing exercises excited her. She seemed to forget all that I had taught her, on those evening rides, and would barely walk a step.

Nicholas was exasperating. He made a point of watching me from his bedroom window, which looked out on the orchard, and he asked endless questions.

"Why doesn't she walk?" he would call.

"Because she's over-excited," I would answer.

"Why's she excited?"

"Because Lydia knocked her about when she schooled her."

"Who's Lydia?"

"Miss Pike."

"Why did Miss Pike knock her about?"

"Because she is a horrible girl with a bad temper."

"If I was Miss Pike's Mummy I would hit her ever so hard. I would make her black and blue. Wouldn't you, Lettie?"

"Yes, I certainly would. Now stop asking questions and let me school in peace."

But it needed Mummy to stop Nicholas. He would never take much notice of me.

During June I schooled Martini four times a week and hacked her twice a week. I kept strictly to a programme when schooling. It was as follows:

Ten minutes walking and trotting on a loose rein, to loosen her up. Thirty minutes balancing exercises at the walk and trot, including work at the ordinary walk, the ordinary, and slow and extended trot, back-reining, halting, turning on the forehand and circling. Five minutes cantering and five minutes walking over a pole on the ground.

Her halting was very bad. She tried to swing her quarters to the right, she snatched at my hands instead of accepting the bit and relaxing her lower jaw, and she stood with her legs all anyhow. Hacking, her tempo seemed good, but in the orchard she was nervous and jumpy, and there was no cadence in her trot. At first she had only to see the pole lying on the ground to start bucking and plunging. In fact she became so upset that I had to dismount and lead her over it in the first two lessons. But gradually she became more sensible and eventually she paid no attention at all. Cantering, she was difficult to control, and several times she tried to take me over the orchard hedge. She was very fussy in the mouth and at times I found it impossible to stop her in a plain snaffle.

The people at Cherryford were very interested in Martini. The baker and the blacksmith gave me advice, and Bob Silver told me to stick to boats. And many were the compliments passed on her appearance. Each day I was encouraged by her improvement. And then something awful happened, which gave Cherryford a topic of conversation for weeks.

It was a Saturday in the third week of June, and for the first time Nicholas was allowed to come riding with me. He could canter now and Pablo although obstinate in the orchard, was very good and obliging on the roads.

It was a gay, windy morning. There were little rustles in the hedgerows and the elms round our house creaked as the wind tossed their branches to and fro. The Lynne was gay with dancing waves and in Duke's Wood a cuckoo called.

"We will go for ever, ever such a long ride, and when we get home we'll be so hungry that we'll eat all the lunch," said Nicholas.

"Don't tire him, Lettie," said Mummy.

We took Tatters with us and went out in high spirits. For a couple of miles we rode quietly by the river. Then we went through the treasured, old-world village of Ferryfields, climbed a long, steep hill and entered the large overgrown woods that lie between Ferryfields and Grayley. Martini was walking well with a long free stride, and every now and then I had to wait for Pablo.

It was a new piece of country to Nicholas and he was so interested that he would not hurry. It was very quiet in the woods; only our hoofs on the hard pathway and the whispering of the wind amongst the trees broke the

127

stillness. Tatters was in heaven. Far below us in the valley he hunted rabbits, but the sound of his voice drifted away from us to the river. Presently we trotted and Martini shied at shadows and birds. On two occasions she all but unseated me. Nicholas thought her very silly.

"Silly old Martini. Fancy being frightened of little things like that. Pablo isn't," he said, and then he started to chant his pet nursery rhyme.

> *"Solomon Grundy*
> *Born on a Monday,*
> *Christened on Tuesday,*
> *Married on Wednesday,*
> *Fell ill on Thursday,*
> *Worse on Friday,*
> *Died on Saturday,*
> *Buried on Sunday,*
> *That was the end of Solomon Grundy."*

And at the same moment Martini began to misbehave. We had reached a windy part of the wood, in full view of a magnificent roll of downs. There was an exhilarating freshness in the air and the great stretch of uncut hay before us rippled like a summer sea. Little clouds raced madly in the deep blue sky. Martini began to sneeze and pull and kick her heels. I sat down hard in the saddle and tried to collect her, but in a plain snaffle it was difficult. Nicholas continued chanting the rhyme. Our pathway ran beside the downs. If we started galloping we could gallop for miles over all those rolling acres of grass and wheat, oats and barley. I could feel Martini tingling as she sniffed the air. I sympathised with her, but I dared not canter in the open country with Pablo and Nicholas. Nicholas, of course, did not realise that I was in difficulties. After he had repeated the wretched nursery rhyme several times, he began to ask me riddles.

"Lettie," he shouted, "how can you say hungry horse in four letters?"

"I don't know and I haven't time to think," I shouted in reply.

"I've *got* you! You don't know. Silly old Lettie. Shall I tell you?"

"Later, when we are home." I used my legs and raised Martini's head to prevent a buck.

"M.T.G.G.," called Nicholas triumphantly.

"Oh, jolly good," I said.

"Why does a thirsty woman carry a watch?" he asked.

"I haven't the foggiest notion," I yelled, trying to straighten Martini, who was dancing sideways, with my legs.

"You might try," pleaded Nicholas.

"Well, catch up. Then I might be able to hear you," I said, hoping that Pablo's presence would calm Martini.

"Okay. Now," said Nicholas, when he had caught up, "why does a thirsty woman carry a watch?"

"So that she knows when the inns are open," I replied.

"Wrong. Wrong. I've got you! You don't know, do you?"

"Because it's got a spring in it. Now I'll ask you another."

"No," I said. "Please don't. Can't you see that I'm having a job with Martini? She's bucking and playing up."

"Why is she bucking?"

"Because the open fields make her want to gallop."

"Why? Why do the open fields make her want to gallop?"

"For goodness' sake, be quiet for a minute or I'll never take you for another ride as long as I live," I said, as Martini gave a whopping buck which nearly sent me over her head.

The remark silenced him for a few moments, and then luckily the pathway turned back into the wood and Martini became calmer. Soon we entered a lane and turned for home through Grayley, which is a little hamlet with a few thatched cottages, a tumbledown farm and a

129

E

well. It was here that Martini first became really frightened; a child was hitting a tin hoop along the lane. It made an awful rattling noise. Martini stopped dead and watched, with quivering nostrils and fast beating heart. Nicholas of course didn't notice her fear.

"What are you stopping for? I'm hungry. Come on," he cried, trotting by.

I shouted at the boy to stop rolling the hoop for a minute, but he didn't hear. Each moment he came nearer and nearer with the terrifying object turning in front of him. Martini stood stock still with arched back, raised tail and shaking sides. Then, as it came within ten yards of her, she swung round and galloped back up the lane as fast as her legs would carry her. At the top by the wood she stopped, and, turning, gazed down to Grayley, where Nicholas and the boy with the hoop were talking. I patted her and lectured her, and then gradually I persuaded her to go back down the lane and past the boy.

"What on earth are you doing? I thought you didn't like galloping in lanes," said Nicholas.

I told him about the hoop and then we walked on in silence. Martini was still nervous. She hesitated at every corner and sidled round every object in the hedgerow.

"She *is* a silly horse," said Nicholas.

"She isn't. She's been knocked about and she's highly-bred and highly-strung," I retorted. I was fed up with Nicholas.

There were fields either side of the lane now, untidy fields with old rusty water troughs and broken carts and tins lying about. Martini found plenty of things to frighten her. She walked with quick springy steps. Then suddenly she stopped dead, turned round and uttered three piercing snorts.

"She's a wild mustang!" said Nicholas.

There were a dozen pigs in the field, fat pink porkers. They were grunting and snuffling in the ground. They looked very greedy and very wicked. Martini stood stock

130

still, her eyes fixed on them. I could feel her heart beating and her flanks heaving. I spoke to her.

"What's the matter now?" asked Nicholas in exasperated accents.

"Pigs," I said, and, as I spoke, all the pigs saw us and of one accord came racing down the field towards us, making the most hideous grunting noises.

I shall never know why they made that charge. Perhaps they thought we were going to feed them. They were a monstrous sight and they shattered Martini's nerves. She gave them one terrified stare and then galloped for home. I sat down hard in the saddle and tried to collect her, but with no avail. I pulled at her mouth. I tried to turn her into the hedge. I said: "Whoa, steady. It's all right. Whoa, whoa, walk, silly, walk, Martini. Pigs won't hurt you," in what I hoped were calming tones. But everything failed. We galloped on.

I had never been so fast before in my life. The fields flashed by. Each moment brought us nearer home. I was a little worried about Nicholas. Looking back, I could see Pablo was following Martini. Nicholas rode jolly well considering his age, but I was afraid he could not stand a long gallop and the ground was hard here for falling, hard and rough with big jagged stones. I tried pulling at Martini until my arms ached, and then I tried sitting still and talking to her. I especially wanted to stop before I reached Cherryford. But as the minutes passed, and Martini's gallop was as fast as ever, my hopes faded. I must say she was a beautiful mover, and if the lane had not been so rough and Nicholas and Pablo had not been following at their own break-neck speed, I think I would have enjoyed the gallop.

Presently we turned a sharp corner and saw Cherryford lying in the valley. Red and brown rooftops, apple blossom, and the river winding silver in the sun. And there was our own pink house, just visible through the trees. What will Mummy say, what will Daddy say, what will Bob Silver say, when Nicholas and I go galloping down the street? I asked myself. And of course I had yet to know the answer. And then the dreaded moment came. I passed the signpost that points to Ferryfields, Longhatch and Greyley, and raced down the street for home. With all my heart I wished our hoofs did not make such a clatter on Cherryford's partly cobbled street. But I wished in vain. Doors and windows were flung wide. People ran to the side of the road out of our way. A car stopped abruptly. Jack Hill, the farrier, hurried to his gate. Mrs. White, the grocer's wife, left her counter. John Hayward left his baking and Bob Silver left his boats. All to see us go clattering by.

"I'm John Gilpin!" cried Nicholas.

Then there was only the bridge between us and home. A child heard our hoofbeats and ran screaming down the road past our house. Three people in a canoe stopped paddling and watched our wild approach. Martini reached the bridge and took it in three bounds. Our white five-barred gate was shut, but she did not hesitate. She jumped and hit the top and fell. And for a moment I saw the drive rising to meet me. And then I had hit the gravel and Martini was lying on my leg—I marvelled at her lightness—and then with a flash of silver shoes she had scrambled to her feet and was standing shaking in the drive. I rose slowly. I was not hurt, but I had to collect my thoughts. I took hold of Martini's rein and patted her. She had scraped her side and one leg.

"Silly girl," I said.

Then I saw Nicholas opening the gate behind me.

"Are you all right, Lettie? I thought you were killed," he said.

Mummy came out of the house with Justice and Jasper at her heels. She had been painting. She still held a palette in one hand and her moygashel slacks had red paint on them. "Whatever on earth are you doing?" she asked.

"We had a bit of a runaway. Some pigs upset Martini. Nicholas was jolly good and galloped all the way from

132

She jumped and hit the top and fell

Grayley. He'll be able to hunt next season. Where's Tatters?" I said.

"Here he comes." said Mummy, and a that moment a very bedraggled Tatters came panting through the gate.

"Poor fellow, you have had a chase, haven't you?"

"What actually happened? Don't be so frightfully mysterious," said Mummy.

"Look, I must bathe Martini. She's got several nasty scratches. Do you mind if I wait and explain at lunch?" I asked

"All right, but buck up," Mummy replied.

CHAPTER EIGHTEEN

MY PARENTS were at first rather alarmed by the tales they heard of my gallop from Grayley to Cherryford. Nicholas gave a vivid description at lunch while I bathed Martini. Mrs. Wise, who scrubs and washes up for us, came hurrying round at two o'clock to find out if either of us had been hurt, and then told Mummy what she had seen.

She said: "I was indoors, dishing up the dinner, when all of a sudden I 'eard their 'oofs come clattering down the road. 'What on earth is that?' I called to Arthur. And then I could tell it was horses like and I ran outside, and there they were tearing down the road like a couple of mad things. Never seen ponies go so fast before, that I 'aven't. Thought they were going straight through Mrs. White's, honest I did. And poor old Nick looked as though he was going to fall off any moment. And then they 'eaded for the river. And I thought, *they've* 'ad it. My 'eart leaped into my mouth as young Lettie galloped up the bridge and then I could see neither 'er nor Nick no more. 'Arthur,' I said to my 'usband, 'directly I've finished my dinner I'm going down to see what's 'appened to them Lonsdales—poor little mites.'"

Bob Silver gave his own special version to Daddy in the street, and on Monday Jim Hayward and Mrs. White compared notes on our doorstep in Mummy's hearing.

But in the end my parents were jolly decent and sensible. They just said that I was not to hack Martini again until she had benefited from another week's schooling in the orchard. I was surprised and pleased by their decision, and on Sunday, filled with hope, I rode her for an hour and a half in the orchard. Then on Monday the weather changed. It rained and rained and rained. And I was sick and had to stay in bed, which was absolutely maddening. Mrs. Wise said I was sick because of my gallop and fall on Saturday. "Delayed shock, that's what it is," she kept saying. Daddy said I was sick because I had eaten too many unripe cherries. Nicholas said I was sick because it was wet and I didn't want to go to school, and Mummy said I was sick because the change of weather had upset me. Meanwhile Martini spent two days resting in the field.

On Wednesday Mummy said I need not go to school, but I was well enough to go out, so I planned to ride Martini in the morning and afternoon.

It was a cold damp day, raw for the time of year and muddy underfoot. The Lynne looked dark and dirty. The trees were still weighed down by the water on the leaves. The skies were dull and grey, and threatened rain.

Directly after breakfast I caught and groomed Martini. The rest had made her nervous again. She jumped whenever I put a hand near her head. She must have been struck over the head at some time or other, for she was always frightened of a raised hand or a riding stick. Mummy, Mrs. Wise and Nicholas came to watch me schooling and their presence filled me with trepidation. Martini was very excited and some time passed before I

135

managed to make her stand still to be mounted. She jogged through the white gate into the orchard with her head and tail very high. She shied and googled at Jasper and Justice, who were lying panting in the grass.

"Be careful now," warned Mummy.

I felt as though I was riding on a spring that would suddenly shoot me high up into the skies. Martini simply would not let me into her back and I was sure that I had never felt so insecure in the saddle before.

"For goodness' sake be careful, duck. She looks wicked this morning," shouted Mrs. Wise.

"She looks terribly fresh," said Mummy.

I shortened my reins and Martini tugged impatiently at my hands. Then she heard a rustle and shot into a gallop. I used my legs and pulled at her mouth, but she stuck her nose in the air and took me to the gate into the stable-yard.

"Do be careful, darling," said Mummy.

"That pony will be the death of you, that she will," called Mrs. Wise.

"Why did you go to the stable-yard?" asked Nicholas.

I turned Martini round, but she didn't want to go back to our schooling corner. She bucked and plunged and ran backwards and pawed the ground.

"Lettie, I think you had better dismount right away," shouted Mummy.

"Else you'll 'ave another accident," added Mrs. Wise.

Suddenly I felt angry. "I'm certainly not going to give in to her. She's going to do as I say," I shouted.

"Ride a cock horse to Banbury Cross," said Nicholas.

"Don't be silly, Nick," said Mummy.

I hit Martini, and she bucked and dug the ground with each front hoof in turn, almost kneeling at the same time.

"You mark my words, that pony's wicked, that she is," called Mrs. Wise.

I used my legs and hit Martini again, and she swung round with a half-rear and faced the gate again. I turned her once more, thinking: This is awful. I must win or

136

they'll make me sell her, and I set into her with my legs. And then suddenly she trotted forward.

"Oh, well done, Lettie. Jolly good. You've won!" cried Mummy. But she spoke too soon. For the next moment Martini heard another rustle in the hedge. She bucked, dropped her near shoulder and then swung round and galloped back towards the gate. The buck unseated me a little and I lost my stirrup, and the swing round threw me on to her neck. I thought: I musn't fall off, I musn't. Then the gallop threw me off all together and I landed on the wet cold grass in a sprawling position.

The next moment Tatters was licking my face, and Jasper and Justice were looking at me with doleful eyes and wrinkled, worried brows.

I leapt to my feet at once, saying: "It's all right, dogs. I'm not hurt."

"Gracious, child, are you badly hurt?" cried Mrs. Wise.

"Are you all right, Lettie?" asked Mummy in calmer tones. "You landed awfully neatly. It was the devil of a buck."

"Yes, I'm all right, thank you," I replied. Then I saw Nicholas had caught Martini (he's always good in an emergency). I mounted her again and started to trot her round the orchard. She was thoroughly excited now and very awkward. Her back was up and she either tugged at the reins or stuck her nose in the air to evade the bit. Again I met with disaster. This time Minnie, our tabby cat, frightened her and she gave three bucks instead of one. I landed on my feet and wrenched my little finger trying to hold on to the reins.

"Lettie," said Mummy, "you've done enough riding for to-day, and that's flat."

"But I can't give in to her," I cried.

"No arguing," said Mummy.

"But you don't understand," I said.

"Yes I do. I understand terribly well. And you are to

137

turn that pony out into the orchard and come indoors at once. It's nearly lunch-time anyway." The firmness of Mummy's voice depressed me.

"Oh, Mummy, don't be mean," whined Nicholas.

"And you can come in and help me fry the omelettes, Nick," she added.

Of course I had to do as I was told. I caught Martini and scolded her, and then I turned her loose and leaned on the gate and looked at the dripping trees and the monotonous grey sky.

It's a miserable day, I thought, and I should hate to try and paint it. I don't wonder Martini was in a miserable mood. One shouldn't ride when the weather is so awful and one had only just recovered from a bilious attack. It shows the lack of imagination.

Then I fell to wondering why Martini was getting worse instead of better. What was I doing wrong? Should I change her bit? She ought to enjoy being ridden Perhaps I was too rough with my hands. I mused until my toes and feet and nose were cold, and then I remembered that I should be laying lunch, and hurried indoors feeling very apprehensive about what Mummy would say on Martini's behaviour.

Mummy said very little and could offer no practicable suggestions, and I felt very depressed.

It started to rain really hard after lunch. There was a leak in our roof and the water came dripping through the ceiling in the passage upstairs, and downstairs we could hear it rushing madly into the well under the scullery floor. Nicholas said:

> "Rain, rain go away,
> Come again another day,
> Nicko wants to make some hay."

Tatters returned soaking wet from a ratting expedition. Jasper and Justice gazed dolefully out of the window. I was sunk in the deepest despair. What *was* I to do with Martini? I collected all of my books on schooling horses and, shutting myself in the morning-room, tried to solve the problem.

It was *Difficult Horses* that first gave me an idea. I found that James Findlay, the author, in his chapter on *Bucking...The Causes and Cure,* gave the following advice: "Several weeks in a drop nose-band and running martingale will often work wonders with a bucker. Used with a plain egg butt snaffle with two reins—the martingale should be fixed to the bottom rein—this combination will put the rider at an advantage and gives him more control than he would have in a double bridle without any danger of the horse becoming constricted or afraid of his mouth."

It was food for thought. I sat thinking in the morning-room till tea-time. The first question which arose was, from where could I borrow a running martingale and drop nose-band? Most children in my predicament would approach their Pony Club, I decided, but I had a guilty conscience where my branch was concerned because I had not attended any rallies during the past year. To tell the truth, I was disheartened by previous experience. You see, I was always put with the "little ones" and instructed by Miss Fipps, a hard-faced, elderly lady with grey hair permanently encased in a most unbecoming net. Miss Fipps was one of the old school. "Lift him, Lettie," she would cry, as I approached a fence. And "Put your legs farther forward and your stirrups right home, and bend your wrists," as I was schooled in the field. And she would tell my parents that my position in the saddle was absolutely incorrect. Once she pulled me out in front of the other "little ones," who were all under ten and said: "Now, this is how you shouldn't sit. You see how Lettie rides. Her reins are too short; her legs are too far back; her feet are not far enough in the stirrups and she sits too far forward in the saddle. If she had to ride a more difficult pony she would come to grief in no time.

139

With her position she couldn't hold a pecking horse up for a moment."

I didn't really mind these criticisms very much because I had complete faith in Pierre St. Denis, who had spent hours correcting my "terrible English seat" and teaching me all that Miss Fipps objected to so strongly. If only I could have been put with the "bigger ones" I think I might have improved, for sometimes they had fairly well-known horsemen to instruct them, but Miss Fipps was sure that neither Pablo nor I were up to cantering circles or jumping anything above one foot high, and so we seemed doomed for ever to her class and I became disheartened.

Sitting now in the morning-room, I recalled long hacks home from rallies, when I had dreamt of the day when Miss Fipps would see me winning the Open Jumping at the White City, or the Prix Caprilli or the British Dressage Championship. But these reminiscences brought no solution to my problem, and presently I fell to thinking of all the people I knew. And then I remembered a girl at my school called Megan O'Connor. She was Irish and her father had several horses, including some youngsters, and most Irishmen use running martingales.

I rang her up after tea and she promised to bring a martingale and drop nose-band to school next day, which was jolly decent, because we were really no more than acquaintances.

During tea I told Mummy that I had found a cure for Martini.

"All right, darling," she said on hearing my plan. "Try it by all means, but be terribly careful. I simply can't bear all this falling off."

"Why did Lettie fall off?" asked Nicholas. "Because she wanted to hit the ground. That's a good one! Mummy, Mummy, don't you think that's a good one?"

"Oh, Nick," said Mummy. "You really are too senseless."

140

"Lettie, why did the chicken cross the road?" asked Nicholas, quite unperturbed.

"Can't remember," I said.

"Got you! 'Cos it wanted to get to the other side, of course. Do you know this one, Lettie? Why did the cow look over the wall?"

"Because it wanted to get to the other side," I replied.

"No silly. 'Cos it couldn't see through. I told you that one yesterday. Do you know this one?"

"No," I interrupted, "and I'm going to go and wash up and make the dogs' dinners."

"Oh, Lettie, you are too mean," wailed Nicholas. "It's such a good one too."

Next day I gobbled my tea even faster than usual, and at five o'clock I was adjusting the martingale and drop nose-band in the stable-yard. I measured the martingale to the withers and adjusted the nose-band so that it was just below the bit and I could fit three fingers between it and the curb groove. Then, full of hope, I mounted and rode into the paddock. I had only Tatters to watch me this evening, for which I was glad.

Martini was fresh, her back was up and she was nervous. She was listening for rustles in the hedge and her eyes were searching for unfamiliar and frightening objects. Presently I told her to trot and then the trouble began. She bucked and swung round and tried to gallop me to the gate. But previously she had succeeded by sticking her nose in the air and opening her mouth, whereas this time I brought the martingale, which forced her head down, into action and the nose-band prevented her opening her mouth as wide as she wished. I lost a stirrup when she bucked, but I quickly regained it, and in a couple of strides I had brought her to a standstill. I was convinced that Martini was not really afraid of anything. She was just playing up. So I made the most of my triumph and, turning her, used my legs and stick and drove her forward in the direction I had first told her to go. We trotted twice round the orchard and then she tried her bucking trick again, but I was ready. I managed to prevent her swinging round, and sent her into a brisk trot. I kept her trotting in the orchard for twenty minutes and then I started schooling her in earnest. I practised transitions from the slow trot to the ordinary trot and the ordinary trot to the extended trot. I practised halting, and circling at the walk and trot. I practised trotting over a pole resting on two boxes and walking in a straight line. She did not attempt to buck again. She responded to the action of the drop nose-band and I began to understand a little how it worked. She would open her mouth to resist the bit when I used the reins, and the nose-band would immediately press on the front of her nose and on the curb groove. She would then drop her nose and relax her lower jaw, and the nose-band would automatically stop pressing her.

I was delighted and, as though sharing my happy mood, the sun came out and a bird, high amongst the apple blossom, burst forth in a song. A window in the house opened and Nicholas' untidy fair head appeared.

"She looks lovely, like the horse in the circus. Look at the sun. I don't see why I should go to silly old bed, it really is too senseless. . . ."

> "The sun has got his hat on,
> Hip, hip, hip, hooray.
> The sun has got his hat on,
> And is coming out to-day."

I thought of coming shows and then I thought of Lydia Pike, who had made Martini so difficult. I remembered that she looked a bad-tempered, lazy girl and I knew she was a very rough rider. Mummy said she was a selfish girl, the sort of daughter who would leave her mother all the washing up to do. I thought of Pip Cox, whom I had met at a children's party and at a gymkhana a year ago.

"Poor Martini," I said, "you've had a rough time of

142

it, haven't you? Never mind, you'll be all right soon."

Then Mummy called that I had forgotten to make the dogs' dinners, so I left the sunlit orchard and turned Martini loose, and went indoors.

CHAPTER NINETEEN

FROM THAT day onwards Martini began to improve. She must have had some concentrated schooling at some earlier time in her life. Perhaps her breaker-in was a wise man. For now she learned very quickly. She stopped fighting against the bit. She became more supple and more attentive to the aids. My parents were very pleased, and soon I started to hack her again.

Then a marvellous thing happened. At the beginning of July my school had an epidemic of measles and had to close. I had all day and every day free for riding.

I was sure that Martini needed plenty of quiet work, so I gave her an hour's schooling and an hour's hacking a day, and within a fortnight she was jumping two feet six out of a trot. She was nervous of triples and parallel bars, but I knew this was Lydia's fault. Lydia had strapped her head down so that she could not extend herself, making it terribly difficult for her to clear any broad obstacles. And Martini had developed a cat-jumping habit, because Lydia did not give her enough freedom over the jumps, and she had become afraid of her mouth. So now I jumped Martini on a very loose rein and soon discarded the martingale, and gradually she became more confident. She lost the habit of kicking whenever she hit a jump, and she lost the habit of rolling back her eyes to see what my stick was doing. She began to look more at her fences when she approached them, and as a result she hit them

143

less often. We had one or two quarrels, but if any difficulties arose or she started to excite herself, and plunge and paw the ground, I always lowered the jumps at once. I found this method very successful.

Mummy and Nicholas were very decent and helped me make fences out of some wood I had bought for very little, with my pocket money, from a nearby woodman. I found some three-ply in the garage and made letters, and marked out a dressage arena, like Pierre St. Denis's arena.

Towards the end of July I recieved my Pony Club's fixture list. They were holding a show and gymkhana on the first of August. I decided to enter Martini for the Equitation and Jumping classes. I told Megan of my decision when I returned her martingale—I was still using the drop nose-band—and she said I could ride over one day and practice over her jumps. I accepted the offer and a week before the show I had a rehearsal at her place. Her fences, built by her father's men, were solid and formidable, but well winged. I was able to take them fairly fast and Martini jumped magnificently. Megan was riding a green youngster, which bucked between the fences and tried to run out. However, she only laughed at his misbehaviour. She was not interested in schooling or dressage or show jumping. She was only interested in hunting and point-to-pointing. Her great ambition was to win a point-to-point.

Then July the thirty-first arrived and I took Martini for a quiet hack in the morning. It was a very hot day. There was hardly a ripple in the river, so slight was the summer breeze, and the flies buzzed ceaselessly round the ponies' heads. The dogs would not venture from the shade of our garden except for a dip in the Lynne. Mummy set out early with her easel, canvas, brushes, paints and palette to start a landscape, a picture of the rolling fields of corn by Grayley, a picture of blue and gold, of sunshine and the clear hot skies.

Nicholas was riding in the egg and spoon race for children under ten at the show, so after lunch I helped him groom and trim Pablo and clean his tack on the condition that he asked no riddles or questions. Pablo and Martini are encouraging ponies to groom, because you can get a wonderful shine on their coats. Soon Pablo shone like polished ebony and Martini shone like polished oak, and by tea-time we had finished grooming them. We kept them in the stable till dusk, because the flies were so awful, when Mummy, who had insisted that I should go to bed at half-past seven, turned them out.

The night was so stiflingly hot that I slept little, and I felt so sleepy when I wakened at six in the morning that I bathed in the river before catching the ponies. It was a wonderful morning. An early haze lay over the fields and the sleeping cottages of Cherryford, but above, the sky was blue and in the east a great golden sun rose slowly, lighting the treetops and the rooftops with gold. A summer breeze, rich and warm, stirred the grasses. In the boughs of the elms and in the green hedges the birds sang their welcome to the day.

And so, I thought, another August begins. A month of holidays and hopes, a month of fêtes and horse shows, of crowded trains and loaded charabancs. For me, this year, a happy and exciting month. And then at once my mind was filled with doubt... would it be happy? Might I not disgrace myself to-day? Gallop like a mad thing from the ring? For a few moments I saw myself as I had seen Lydia at the Stringwell Show, and then, in my imagination I heard Daddy say, "The pony must go, Lettie. She'll only break your neck. I'm sorry, but there it is," and I felt a wave of disappointment and sadness, a sickening tug at the heart. And then I remembered that this was only make-believe. The show was not over but soon to begin. I must hurry, not waste time in dismal day-dreams.

I ran indoors and changed from my bathing dress to my shorts and aertex shirt and sandshoes. A moment later I was in the orchard catching the ponies, which were damp with dew and sleepy-eyed. There were two rabbits nibbling the short sweet grass under the white heart tree, and Tatters, yapping wildly, chased them to their burrows. It was the first sharp penetrating noise to shake the morning air, and it made me wide awake at last.

I washed the ponies' tails and presently Nicholas came out from the house.

"I say," he said. "I'm awfully sure I shall be last. My hand's shaking. I shall never, hold a spoon."

"Nonsense. Come and help me groom. Grooming will make your hand steady again," I told him.

At eight o'clock I started plaiting the ponies' manes. I am not nimble with my fingers, and my plaits looked loose and floppy. Martini made matters worse by constantly shaking her head. Nicholas asked questions until in exasperation I sent him in to breakfast, and Tatters yapped and yapped because Minnie was up a tree and for some unknown reason he doesn't think Minnie should be allowed to climb trees. By nine o'clock I was nearly demented. I vowed secretly that I would never again enter for a horse show and I snapped at Mummy when she called, "Breakfast," for the fourth time.

At long last I was indoors eating and dressing. I recited poetry to take my mind off the Equitation Class.

> *"I strove with none, for none was worth my strife.*
> *Nature I loved, and, next to nature, Art:*
> *I warm'd both hands before the fire of life;*
> *It sinks and I am ready to depart."*

I felt that I had already striven too long. Why do I strive? I wondered. Why not stay at home whenever possible, in peace and quiet?

I wondered how other children felt before horse shows. Did they wish they had never entered?

And then it was time to go.

It was a long, hot ride to the show ground, and the ponies were very quiet. We had two miles of roadwork at the start, and very dusty miles they were too, and

146

then we took a bridle path that led us through the fields high in corn and pasture that smelt of burnt grass and hot clover, and a fir-wood that smelt dry and harsh as all fir-woods do. After a little while we reached a rough hill-side dotted with gorse and broom, and we dismounted and rested the ponies, for Pablo was showing signs of weariness. There came to us the scent of thyme and the hum of bees, and, from the tall bitter grass, the burr of grasshoppers. We looked down into the valley where we had ridden only a few moments before, to the rolling acres of gold and the brown pastures, to the winding track, dusty and grey, which had guided us so faithfully towards our destination. And we looked to the horizon of blue, to the deep blue sky.

"What colours!" I cried. "They are like Van Gogh's Provence. Never have I seen such gold before. How I wish I could paint! Or even write."

"Oh, that reminds me. Do you know this one, Lettie? Why is an author a queer animal?" asked Nicholas.

"I don't know," I said without troubling to think. "Gosh, it's a quarter to eleven and we've two miles to go. We must push on."

"Because his tale comes out of his head," said Nicholas.

"Whose? Oh—the author's—sorry. That's quite a good one. Come on. Hop up."

A mile of grassland and twenty minutes' ride down lanes and roads bought us to the show ground, where the first class, an Equitation Competition for children under ten, was in progress. Mummy and Daddy had arrived. I could see our three dogs and our battered car over by the Collecting Ring. Bob Saunders, who is a Pony Club member though he never attends rallies, was cantering Nobby Boy in circles. Nicholas dismounted.

"Poor Pablo's tired already," he said.

Mummy appeared panting at my side.

"Lettie, you are terribly late. Do hurry. Your class is is next," she said.

"We had to stop on the way, 'cos Pablo was tired.

We've had a lovely ride, Mummy, through corn and hayfields. We've come ever, ever such a long way," said Nicholas.

I loosened Martini's girths, took her to the car and brushed her over and oiled her feet. When I mounted the megaphone was calling all competitors for Class Two trotting circles, and then I realised that I was riding in a snaffle and drop nose-band instead of the double bridle as I had intended. I cantered back to the car and, with Nicholas's help, changed my bridle, and then it was time to enter the ring. Miss Fipps was at the entrance.

"What's that you are riding? Not a bad-looking brute, is it?" she asked.

I paused.

"Yes, I think she's quite nice-looking, but I don't know how she'll behave," I answered.

"What have you done with that dreadful little black animal?" she called, but I was walking into the ring, and because I thought her remark about dear little Pablo rude I pretended not to hear.

There were two judges, both men. They were not the usual ones we have for our Pony Club Show, in fact I was sure I had never seen them in my life before. There were about fifteen competitors in the class, which was open to members of ours and our neighbouring Pony Clubs; nearly all of them rode with their legs well forward. Presently we were told to trot and then to canter. We were going round to the right and three riders were sent out of the ring because they were leading with the wrong leg. Fortunately Martini was calm, and when she is calm she never makes a mistake when told to canter. Presently we were sent round on the other rein and four more riders were asked to leave the ring because they led off on the wrong leg. Then the eight of us that remained were lined up. The oldest judge, who wore spectacles and looked too old and decrepit to ride, explained that he wanted each of us in turn to trot up to the brush fence and canter back on the off leg, and then halt in front of his co-judge and himself, and rein-back three steps.

Maureen Fielding, a red-haired girl who, according to Miss Fipps, has a perfect seat, went first. She bent her pony's head outwards when she turned at the brush fence and pulled on the reins when she backed, relaxing her hands for a second each time the pony took a step. Next a boy on a piebald tried the test and was sent out because he could not make his pony canter. He was followed by a tall elegant girl on an obviously schooled and balanced hunter. I thought she rode well, with a style that would have pleased Pierre St. Denis. Her horse gave an excellent show. He carried himself with an air; he flexed his head inwards when he turned the corner and led straight off at the canter. Someone whispered that the tall girl came from a pony club in Oxfordshire or Berkshire and that she had been placed in dressage tests. Now it was my turn. A steward beckoned to me. For an awful moment I panicked; I could not remember what I was supposed to do. I looked helplessly at the judges and then suddenly the test came back to me. I collected my thoughts, shortened my reins and trotted up to the brush fence. Martini was nervous and hesitant and as a result, she was not trotting straight. I used my legs and then, as we turned, I lowered my outside hand and used my outside leg just behind the girth and my inside leg on the girth. She led off correctly, and with a feeling of tremendous relief I cantered back to the judges. Although I used my legs, she was rather on the forehand when I halted and she did not back quite straight. However, the old judge looked fairly pleased and said, "Well done," which was heartening.

Only four riders survived the test. The others were sent out for not cantering at all or for leading off on the wrong leg.

Presently we were told that we were to trot and canter a circle to either hand. I began to feel sick so I didn't watch my fellow-competitors. Instead I looked at the spectators They were a drab crowd on the whole. Mummy was the only gaily-dressed adult that I could see. She was wearing a plain yellow-checked frock and a blue jacket and a large straw hat from Sorrento. Miss Fipps was wearing a very dreary coat and skirt; it drooped terribly and its colour bore a strong resemblance to mud. I fell to wondering why she liked such dreary shades. And then the tall girl said: "The judges want you to go next," and with horror I realised that I had been sitting gaping at the ringside while the decrepit judge had been speaking to me.

"I'm terribly sorry," I said, hurrying Martini away from the other ponies.

"All right," the younger judge said. "Take it easy. Don't get fussed."

Martini went well with a nice even tempo at the trot, but, cantering, she rushed a little and my circle became larger than I intended. She was a little worse to the right than the left, and at one moment she was very heavy on on my hands. I decided that I might be placed fourth and wondered vaguely whether my rosette would be white or green and whether it would say fourth or reserve. Then I looked at the judges and noticed that the other riders were moving.

"Come on," said the tall girl. "You've got second."

I hurried forward and stood beside her, making Martini look as nice as I could.

"Your pony goes well into her bridle. And her tempo's good. Give her some more schooling and then try her in some Elementary or Novice Dressage Tests later on. She might win something. Where did you learn, by the way?" said the decrepit judge, handing me a blue rosette.

"Thanks awfully. Pierre St. Denis taught me all I know about dressage. I think he's frightfully good," I told him and wished I hadn't said *awfully* and *frightfully*.

"You lucky girl!" said the younger judge.

"Couldn't find a much better instructor," remarked the decrepit judge.

"Thanks frightfully," I said, and then, as I couldn't think of anything else to say, I turned and followed the tall girl who had won first and cantered round the ring. I had an awful desire to grin broadly, but I quelled it because I did not wish to appear triumphant or smug or self-satisfied.

In many ways it is easier to be a good loser than a good winner. I have so often lost in races and competitions that I never expect to win, and therefore I am never disappointed or annoyed when I lose.

My parents were very surprised by my success. Daddy had not watched all the Equitation Class, and he was amazed to see my blue rosette.

"Good lord!" he said. "You don't mean to say you've *won* something. Janet, Janet, Lettie's actually won something. Old Miss Fripps will die of shock."

"Not Fripps, *Fipps*. I think Martini's been jolly clever," I said.

Mummy gave Martini six lumps of sugar, and then the megaphone called me into the Collecting Ring for the Children's Jumping. There were nine entries in this class including Bob Saunders with Nobby Boy.

Pierre St. Denis would not have approved of the course. The jumps were narrow and flimsy and fell too easily. But the Pony Club members liked them, because they were well winged. Because the Pony Club members rode with their legs too far forward, they could never keep their ponies straight at unwinged obstacles. Two of the older members were complaining now about the judges.

"Can't think why Miss Fipps asked such awful judges. One of them is not even English. And he learned at some cavalry school in France. Like to see him hunting in this country."

"Don't worry, Jane, he wouldn't. He would be scared of the fences. But I know why Miss Fipps got them. It's this Pony Club Inter-Branch Competition. They are experts on that sort of thing and she wants to know what they think of us."

The standard of jumping was very low, and the first two competitors each had three refusals and were disqualified. Then Bob Saunders jumped his usual clear round with Nobby Boy. He's a very rough rider, but he's fairly successful with his cobs. Then it was my turn. Martini was nervous and up to now I had kept her walking about. She was trembling when I entered the ring. I remembered Lydia's dramatic exit at Stringwell, and decided to take her slowly. The first jump was a brush fence. I took it from a trot and then increased to a canter for the second—a pair of hurdles—and then slowed down for the third—a gate—which was the nearest to the exit and entrance.

As Martini landed she tried to put on a spurt, but I was ready and collected her in time. We passed the entrance at a slow canter and knocked the stile, which was the fourth jump and very flimsy indeed. Only three more remained: some rails, a very poor imitation of a red brick wall and a narrow triple. We cleared them all, and faint applause accompanied us from the ring.

Outside, I dismounted and patted Martini. Mummy came hurrying across the show ground. Nicholas was waiting for the egg and spoon race, which was the next event. I could hear him talking to the tall girl, whom he admired tremendously. He was saying: "Why did the chicken cross the road?"

I wished he would not bother people with his silly riddles.

"Well done, Lettie." said Mummy. "You were terribly good."

"I took her too slowly at the stile. It was my fault she hit it," I said

Presently I loosened Martini's girths and lay in the long grass looking at the cloudless sky. I thought: I mustn't forget this day; it's one of the happiest in my life. I don't mind if I don't win anything in the jumping. I know she's improving and that's all that matters. One day I'm going to school some of the best horses in England. I'm going to be an expert. To-day is the first step up the ladder to success.

I was surprised when I was handed the blue rosette

And I gazed at Martini and thought: She's lovely. Look at those long forearms and those neat short cannon bones. Look at her head, so well-bread and intelligent. I wish I could paint horses.... I'm really the luckiest child here. No one else has such a marvellous pony.

I was so hot that I couldn't watch the other competiters, but I had seen most of them jump at rallies and I knew they were not particularly good. I was not unprepared when I heard my number called over the megaphone. This time I was half-expecting to win second or third, though I was surprised when I was handed the blue rosette and I realised that I had beaten the tall girl, who told me that she had knocked the rails and stile. We cantered round the ring and then Bob Saunders, the winner, shoved Nobby Boy into a cattle-truck and dashed off to another show.

I ate lunch while the egg and spoon race was in progress Nicholas was last in his heat, because he dropped his egg three times.

Then, after Nicholas and the ponies had eaten—Martini waited for Pablo—we left for home.

Nicholas was cheerful. "Never mind," he said. "I expect I shall win something one day. P'raps when I'm an old, old man. And now you've got enough to buy Martini a bridle, haven't you? With the three pounds you've won?"

We rode very slowly, because the weather was so hot, and it was past tea-time when we reached home.

CHAPTER TWENTY

TOWARDS EVENING the telephone rang. I answered and a voice the other end said Miss Fipps wanted to speak to Lettie Lonsdale.

"Lettie speaking," I replied.

"Oh, yes, well," said Miss Fipps. "You know the older of the two judges to-day? He's my brother-in-law. He's got all sorts of crazy notions about riding—always did have them. Thinks you should lean forward down-hill ... simply ridiculous.... But he's supposed to be an expert on this dressage stuff. So I told him to come to-day and judge and tell me who was best to ride in a team for this Dressage Championship—Branch Competition or whatever it's called. Never could remember the name of the wretched thing. Anyway, he picked on you, first of everyone. Likes your pony. Say's she's well schooled and can jump and he'll train you. Are you interested? Seems to me simply ridiculous—all this bothering about angles and flexions and cadence. What does it all matter as long as the horse goes?" She paused for breath.

154

"I should love to be trained," I said quickly.

"He says we must enter a team even though the other two won't have a chance. But you can ride as an individual as well. He thinks you might have a chance —might get high marks or something," said Miss Fipps.

"When do I start being trained?" I asked.

"He's staying with me and you're to come the day after to-morrow."

"By the way, what is his name?"

"Peter Venten. He's Belgian, you know. I suppose that's why he has such odd ideas."

"Not the author of *The Training of Mount and Man*?" I asked.

"Yes, I think his book's called something like that."

"But that's wonderful!" I cried.

"Well he will give you three weeks' teaching. Good-bye," said Miss Fipps, and she rang off abruptly.

For a moment I sat quite still holding the telephone.

Peter Venten, I thought. The Belgian expert! It's too good to be true. . . . Three weeks' training—and he thinks I have a chance. . . . Pierre thinks a lot of Venten. . . . It's like a dream, a marvellous dream.

Mummy's voice came to me. "Anyone interesting?" she called. I ran upstairs and told her all. "The Pony Club Inter-Branch Competition! It's marvellous," I finished.

"Some people are born with silver spoons in their mouths," said Mummy.

Nicholas came out of his bedroom in his pyjamas. He said: "Who was born with a silver spoon? Not Grundy.

Solomon Grundy
Born on a Monday,
Christened on Tuesday,
Married on Wednesday,
Fell ill on Thursday,
Worse on Friday,

155

Died on Saturday,
Buried on Sunday,
That was the end of Solomon Grundy."

"I'm going to tell Martini," I said.

"Give Pablo an apple and a pat from me. It wasn't his fault we were last," said Nicholas.

I went outside and looked down to the river. The last pale light of day lay on the water-meadows. A solitary swan, white as snow, paddled by our lawn. The scent of hot earth and burnt grass lingered on the evening air.

I wandered to the orchard and found Martini and Pablo grazing side by side. They raised their heads at the sound of my voice and, while they ate apples from my hand, listened to my story of days to come.

"You see," I finished, "I've lots to learn. But this is the beginning. When I am seventeen or eighteen I shall compete at Badminton. Later I shall jump for England on a horse that I have trained myself."

I saw a show ring in Paris, by Autieul. The white jumps with green shrubs either side; the stands decked with flowers; the chic Parisian spectators with exotic hats and gay accessories. I saw Rome, as I had read of her. The great quiet churches; the priests with long robes and sandals on their feet; St. Peter's; the jangling trams in the main streets; the Tiber, hot and muddy in the summer sun.

"I shall take a day off to look at pictures," I said.

But the ponies were no longer listening, they had left me and were grazing under the white heart tree.

The air was cooler now and night was falling. The sky was a dark and inky blue with one brave star shining high above our tallest elms. I thought: For years we strive to satisfy our vanity, to achieve our small ambitions, to shine in the eyes of others or better the world. But all the great things are here without the asking. The silhouette of a tree against the starry sky; early sunlight on hills; the ripple of river water between fingers; springtime in England and the song of the birds. And yet these are not enough. There is for ever the urge to improve and create.

"And all my life," I told the sleeping orchard, "I shall paint pictures and improve horses."

Armada's Pony Parade

A host of exciting books about the wonderful world of horses and ponies are available in colourful Armada paperbacks. Each one, by a popular author and with a striking cover picture, makes a prize addition to your collection. Whether you have a pony of your own, or can only dream of one, they are all stories to thrill you.

Go galloping through the many pony adventures by the famous **Pullein-Thompson** sisters, **Christine, Diana** and **Josephine.**

Read about the escapades of Georgie and her beautiful chestnut pony, Spot, in the series by **Mary Gervaise.**

Ride into excitement and danger with Jackie, the daring young heroine of the pony series by **Judith Berrisford.**

There are so many different titles to collect. You can build up your own Pony Parade. If you would like a list of all the pony books now available, send a stamped, self-addressed envelope to :

Armada Books,
14 St. James's Place,
London SW 1A 1PF

We will send you a complete Armada stocklist.

The Armada Quiz and Puzzle Books
Nos. 1-5

Boost your brain power and have hours of puzzling fun solving the hundreds of different quizzes in this popular Armada series.

Pick your favourite puzzle – names, pictures, anagrams, codes, magic squares, pets, mysteries, sport, history, spelling, doodles, and many, many more. Sharpen your wits and get puzzling!

Have you discovered Armada's latest quiz books? Facts and fun for everyone in six exciting titles:

The Armada Horse & Pony Quiz Books Nos. 1 & 2
by Charlotte Popescu

The Armada Football Quiz Books Nos. 1 & 2
by Gordon Jeffery

The Armada Animal Quiz Book
by Deborah Holder

Car Quiz
by Hal Danby

Armada

Armada books are chosen by children all over the world. They're designed to fit your pocket, and your pocket money too – why not build up your own Armada library? There are hundreds of exciting titles and favourite series to collect, and their bright spines look marvellous on any bookshelf. Armada have something for everyone:

Books by popular authors like **Enid Blyton – Malcolm Saville – Elinor Brent-Dyer – Alfred Hitchcock**, etc.

The best mysteries and most exciting adventure stories.

Favourite characters like **Jennings – William – Nancy Drew – The Hardy Boys – Biggles – The Three Investigators – The Lone Piners** – and many, many more.

Pony books by the Pullein-Thompson sisters, Mary Gervaise and Judith Berrisford.

A wonderful collection of famous children's stories.

Ghost books to make your hair stand on end!

A terrific collection of **quiz, puzzle and fun books** to entertain you for hours.

These are just a few of the good things Armada has in store for you.

If you'd like a complete up-to-date list of Armada books, send a stamped, addressed envelope to:

> Armada Books,
> 14 St James's Place,
> London SW1.